WHAT DO YOU THINK?

Preparing for the Question That All Clients Ask

WHAT DO YOU THINK?

Preparing for the Question That All Clients Ask

BRADLEY M. SMITH FSA, MAAA

Library of Congress Cataloging-in-Publication Data

Smith, Bradley M.
What do you think? : preparing for the question that all clients ask / Bradley M. Smith.
p. cm.
Includes bibliographical references and index.
ISBN 978-0-9759337-4-9 (alk. paper)
1. Actuaries--Vocational guidance. 2. Business ethics. 3. Employment interviewing. I. Title.
HG8781.S627 2010
650.1--dc22

2010006065

ISBN 978-0-9759337-4-9

First Edition

Printed in the United States of America

17 16 15 5 6 7 8 9

Contents

Acknowledgements

With deepest appreciation I would like to thank Jim Loughman and Jeremy Engdahl-Johnson for their help in editing this piece. They made me look substantially more articulate than I am.

Thanks to Jennifer Washburn, my assistant, for helping me with the logistics of everyday life as a consultant.

I would also like to thank my many friends and colleagues, both past and present, at Milliman. Working with the best has brought the best out in me.

Finally, I would like to thank my wife, Karen and my daughter, Emily. This book reflects lessons hard learned over a consulting career. Those lessons take a toll on everyone, particularly those closest to the individual learning them. Thank you for your love and life-long support.

About the Author

BRADLEY M. SMITH, FSA, MAAA

Brad Smith is a graduate of the University of Illinois, a Fellow of the Society of Actuaries and a member of the American Academy of Actuaries. Brad joined Milliman, Inc. in 1986. He is a principal of the firm and has served as its chairman since May, 2000. As a consultant he specialized in the pricing and design of new products. Additionally, he assisted potential acquirers of life insurance companies with mergers and acquisitions.

Brad is a frequent speaker and has authored a number of papers. He is a co-author of the book *US GAAP for Life Insurers, 2nd edition* published by the Society of Actuaries. He has served as a board member and vice president on the Board of Directors of the Society of Actuaries and is an emeritus board member of The Actuarial Foundation, having served as its vice chairman. He has been married to Karen since 1977. They have one daughter, Emily.

Introduction

As chairman of an international consulting firm with diverse service offerings, I am often asked to speak before a variety of groups. On a fairly regular basis, I have addressed young professionals in our company who are just beginning their consulting careers. On other occasions the audience included experienced, seasoned professionals. Outside the consulting arena, I have enjoyed the opportunity to speak to students, ranging from high school to graduate school. The essence of my messages to these groups is contained in this book. While the focus is on consulting, many of the messages can easily be extrapolated and have meaning in the context of employment as a professional within the corporate world. Thus, "consultant" in this context should be interpreted broadly to mean any professional who offers advice to an interested constituency. For those entering their consulting careers, I hope this book gives you insight into what you can expect. For veteran consultants, I hope my messages resonate with you and are not so simplistic as to insult you in any way. Please consider this volume as "batting practice;" preparing you, or reminding you, of the sometimes difficult challenges you face on an everyday basis.

Brad Smith

DO YOU THINK? WHAT DO YOU THINK? WHAT DO YOU THINK? WHAT DO
YOU THINK? WHAT DO YOU THINK? WHAT DO YOU THINK? WHAT DO YOU
THINK? WHAT DO YOU THINK? WHAT DO YOU THINK? WHAT DO YOU TH
T DO YOU THINK? WHAT DO YOU THINK? WHAT DO YOU THINK? WHAT D
DO YOU THINK? WHAT DO YOU THINK? WHAT DO YOU THINK? WHAT DO
YOU THINK? WHAT DO YOU THINK? WHAT DO YOU THINK? WHAT DO YOU
THINK? WHAT DO YOU THINK? WHAT DO YOU THINK? WHAT DO YOU TH
T DO YOU THINK? WHAT DO YOU THINK? WHAT DO YOU THINK? WHAT D
DO YOU THINK? WHAT DO YOU THINK? WHAT DO YOU THINK? WHAT DO

SUCCEEDING IN YOUR CAREER

THINK? WHAT DO YOU THINK? WHAT DO YOU THINK? WHAT DO YOU TH
T DO YOU THINK? WHAT DO YOU THINK? WHAT DO YOU THINK? WHAT D
DO YOU THINK? WHAT DO YOU THINK? WHAT DO YOU THINK? WHAT DO
YOU THINK? WHAT DO YOU THINK? WHAT DO YOU THINK? WHAT DO YOU
THINK? WHAT DO YOU THINK? WHAT DO YOU THINK? WHAT DO YOU TH
T DO YOU THINK? WHAT DO YOU THINK? WHAT DO YOU THINK? WHAT D
DO YOU THINK? WHAT DO YOU THINK? WHAT DO YOU THINK? WHAT DO
YOU THINK? WHAT DO YOU THINK? WHAT DO YOU THINK? WHAT DO YOU
THINK? WHAT DO YOU THINK? WHAT DO YOU THINK? WHAT DO YOU TH

ONE

THE QUESTION THAT ALL CLIENTS ASK

There is one question that all clients ask. It is not, "What will it cost?" or "How long will it take?" although many clients do ask those questions. Rather, the question that all clients ask a consultant is, "What do you think?"

What do you think we should charge for this product? What do you think the return on investment will be? How much do you think we should set aside to fund this obligation? What do you think?

There are many layers of complexity to that seemingly simple, four-word question that all clients ask, and your ability to master each layer goes a long way toward determining if you will be successful. Even before you start, the first requirement is that you must be an expert on a topic that the client cares about. Anyone who wants a successful professional consulting career must possess a high degree of expertise, intelligence and proven ability in his or her specialty. If you lack this requirement, eventually you will fail.

A second aspect of the question that all clients ask is the client's perception of you as a professional. He must know (or have strong reason to believe) that you are an expert. The landscape is littered with "closet" experts; consultants who are very well versed in a particular area, yet they have failed. If the marketplace does not know you are an expert in your specialty area, you might never even get the opportunity to answer the question that all clients ask.

The third requirement to successfully answer the question that all clients ask is your ability to communicate your answer in a readily-understood, straightforward manner. In other words, you must not expect or require that the client will possess the same level of expertise that it took for you to formulate your answer. If you cannot simplify the issues surrounding the question and articulate the reasons for your conclusions, you may not have as much expertise in the area as you believe you do. If you are not an effective communicator, you almost certainly will not be asked back again to answer the question that all clients ask.

The final consideration to the question that all clients ask, and what should be the most obvious, is that you must be able to think in the context of the client's requirements. The world has become a very complicated place. There are precious few "cookie cutter" solutions that actually work. Rather, each solution must be tailored to the particular client's situation. This may sound simplistic and obvious. However, you would be surprised at how many new, young professionals find this task enormously difficult.

I remember one young consultant. He was very bright and possessed good communication skills. However, like many beginning professionals, he was very "process oriented." It was not unusual for me to ask a question and for him to go off and develop a computer model that would enable him to answer the question. After a few days he would return with the computer output which, in his mind, contained the answer. With one look I could tell that there was something wrong with what he produced. When I asked if he checked the result, the answer would always be "Yes," even though many times it would be obvious that he had not even bothered to look at his results. In his mind he had "checked" the work, because he had reviewed the process he used to perform the analysis. In fact, before (and even after) performing the analysis, he had not given any thought to what useful information his efforts might produce.

Eventually, we both became very frustrated. Finally, we sat down and discussed what was truly expected of him as a consultant. Specifically, he was expected to consider the question and think about the range of results he could expect, rather than merely sitting down and mindlessly running a computer model that may or may not have an input error or actually be appropriate for the task at hand. When told that the job required that he think, he looked directly at me and in all seriousness said the following:

"I don't want to have to think every day of my life. It is too hard!"

I couldn't believe what I was hearing. Here was a person who was blessed with the intellect to address very complicated issues. Questions that others would pay him a great deal of money to answer. Yet, because it was too hard, he didn't want to be burdened with it. To be sure, he wanted to be paid as if he had thoroughly considered the tasks at hand. I was flabbergasted. My response was along the lines of:

"Hard! You believe that thinking is hard! It is not hard. You are blessed with a superior intellect and great potential. 'Hard' is working road construction in Chicago, Illinois when it is 10 degrees outside.

'Hard' is working hot tar roofing when it is 103 degrees in Dallas, Texas. 'Hard' is being 19 years old, shipped 5,000 miles from home to have some stranger shoot tracer bullets at you."

Needless to say, his consulting career with us was very limited.

So, this begs the question. When was the last time you invested in expanding your expertise? The "shelf life" for many professional skills, given the rapidity with which the world is changing, is constantly decreasing. The expertise that you have to offer is being amortized. If you are not regularly re-investing in this amortizing asset, you will become irrelevant to your client base and may eventually wake up to find fewer and fewer people asking you the question that all clients ask.

Of course, every successful consultant is busy answering the questions that are being asked today. It is difficult to find the time to make the investment that is necessary to keep one's expertise relevant. Nonetheless, finding a way to do so is key to enjoying a long career. Over the years I have seen, time and again, that unless consultants develop a disciplined plan to make an ongoing investment in learning, time will pass, and expertise will wane. Set a specific time aside each day, each week, each month in which you will focus on refreshing your existing skills and developing new ones.

Some professionals assume that I am talking here about developing technical skills. Certainly, expertise is a necessary ingredient to a successful professional career. However, effective oral and written communication skills are equally critical. Many professionals are lacking in these areas and consider them to be "soft" skills not worthy of their attention. This is a natural mistake. In reality, most of us tend to practice skills that we are already good at and enjoy, rather than developing capabilities that we are lacking and find tedious or difficult.

Focusing on improving your weaknesses rather than your strengths will enhance the overall return you receive on the investment you make.

Another question: When was the last time you communicated your expertise to your marketplace? Having expertise is one critical ingredient to enjoying a successful career. However, an equally important ingredient is making sure that others know about your expertise. So, when was the last time you wrote an article for publication? Gave a speech? Visited a client to discuss a new idea? Attended an industry conference? Performed independent research? Qualifying yourself as an expert in the client's mind is the first step to being hired.

This will become even more important in the future. Personal productivity, even at the senior levels, is what defines a successful consultant. In the past, success was often defined by the degree to which consultants could leverage their junior staff. However, today it is becoming clear that clients demand and are willing to pay senior consultants who possess high-level expertise. Increasingly, clients demand the value that senior consultants personally bring to the table. They are less willing to pay for support staff to perform functions that can be executed, less expensively and more efficiently, by their own in-house staff. This trend is reflected in the decreasing staff leverage, defined as total professionals per principal/partner, in many professional services firms. Additionally, the emergence of personal productivity tools and software, whether spreadsheets, word processing, e-mail, voicemail, cell phones or BlackBerries has reduced the need for support staff. All of this points to the increasing importance of developing your expertise and communicating it to the marketplace.

TWO

INTEGRITY

At the end of 2005 an article was published in the *Wall Street Journal* identifying the 10 "most-searched-for words" on the Internet. Thinking about what had transpired during the year, including Hurricane Katrina and the papal election, made some of those words obvious choices. "Levee," "tsunami," "refugee," "pandemic" and "conclave" all made the list. However, the most requested word for searches on the Web in 2005 was something else entirely: "integrity." This led many pundits to crack jokes about society searching for integrity on the Web. At the risk of being so accused, I searched for the word "integrity." I found over 109 million links, including some commercial enterprises selling used cars or offering unsecured loans. Many modern day philosophers have attempted to define integrity. Likewise, it is clear that many college professors find "integrity" to be a worthy topic for publication. After reading many of the entries, I decided that the most appropriate definition for integrity is "doing the right thing, even when no one is watching."

This is particularly important in our firm, where election as a principal requires that the individual possesses integrity. It is difficult to prove to someone you do not know well that you have integrity. It is the result of the sum total of actions and choices made throughout a lifetime. However, it takes only one or two bad choices to illustrate a lack of integrity.

I have come to the conclusion that cycles are natural phenomena in many aspects of both life and business. Economic cycles are well documented, as are pricing cycles that result in both hard and soft markets in insurance, real estate and finance. I'll leave it to the psychologists to explain why behavioral cycles occur, but their existence is difficult to dispute.

I raise this issue because I believe that we are now experiencing, for lack of a better phrase, an ethical cycle. More specifically, I believe that we are witnessing an increasing lack of tolerance by the public for ethical lapses on the part of its public figures, whether business leaders, political leaders or school teachers. This intolerance for unethical behavior reached a low in the late 1990s and early 2000s. That is, as a society, we tolerated an increasing degree of unethical behavior during that time period.

The greatest danger in most cycles is that people will do exactly the opposite of what they should do, and at the worst possible time. Obvious examples include making substantial capital investments at the peak of an economic boom period or failure to make the necessary investment at the end of an economic downturn, just as markets are beginning to turn upward.

I believe the same danger awaits in a cycle of intolerance of unethical behavior. Examples include the indictments of business leaders in the insurance brokerage scandal, the accounting for bogus reinsurance deals, the Martha Stewart insider trading fiasco or the backdating of the issuance of stock options. In each of those examples and many others we heard a common refrain.

Everyone is doing it.

In some cases it certainly appears that many were, in fact, "doing it." Practices that have been criticized by those outside of the insurance brokerage industry were, regrettably, all too commonplace within the industry. The same can be said of the accounting for some reinsurance transactions. The Financial Times estimated that 100 companies would be affected by the backdating of stock options issued to executives of those companies.

What is apparent in each of these incidents is the danger of "incestuous" and "incremental" thinking. Here are a few examples.

BID RIGGING

Within the insurance brokerage industry the practice of incentive compensation has been embedded and accepted for a long time. This led to compensation arrangements between brokers and insurance companies in which brokers would be paid more for each incremental piece of business if their overall production with the company increased. Since brokers are typically retained by the purchasers of insurance products these incentive compensation arrangements called the brokers' independence into question, especially when the compensation arrangements were not disclosed to their clients. Eventually, this led some brokers to rig bids in favor of certain carriers from which the broker received incremental compensation. Few, if any, outside the industry believe that bid rigging is an acceptable, ethical practice. However, through a step-by-step process, too many of those within the insurance industry came to rationalize such a practice, primarily because it benefited them.

OPTIONS BACKDATING

Nothing illustrates this phenomenon better than the apparently all-too-common practice of backdating the stock options issued to corporate executives. A little background may be beneficial. Stock options are issued to company executives to align their interests with those of the company's shareholders. If the company's share price goes up the shareholders obviously benefit. By issuing "at the money" stock options to executives, their compensation increases if the stock price increases. "At the money" options are those having a strike price equal to the price of the stock on the day it was issued. "In the money" options are those having a strike price below the price of the stock on the day it was issued.

Stock options are typically issued on either a regular basis, meaning their issuance is tied to a certain date, or on an irregular basis, meaning their issuance is at the discretion of either the company's board or their compensation committee. Some would argue that the issuance of stock options on an irregular basis is fraught with the potential for unethical behavior. For instance, the irregular issuance of stock options would allow them to be granted at times when the stock is artificially low. One oft-cited example is the issuance of stock options shortly after a national crisis, such as the terrorist attacks on the United States on September 11, 2001.

The flap over the issuance of stock options was not an example of this issue. Rather, it seemed that some company officials were not satisfied with issuing options on the dates that the stock price appeared to be artificially low. Instead, they waited until they knew the date during the preceding year on which the stock price was actually at its lowest! Essentially, they were issuing themselves "in the money" options. This, in and of itself, is not illegal, although it clearly is not consistent with the stated objective of offering incremental compensation for an increasing stock price. Falsely representing that these options were issued "at the money" is deceptive, unethical and caused the accounting for the cost of the options to be reflected inaccurately in the company's financial statements. What follows is an excerpt from a "Page One" story in the *Wall Street Journal* on March 18, 2006, entitled "Some CEOs reap millions by landing stock options when they are most valuable. Luck or something else?"

> *On Oct. 13, 1999, William W. McGuire, CEO of giant insurer UnitedHealth Group Inc., got an enormous grant in three parts that – after adjustment for later stock splits – came to 14.6 million options. So far, he has exercised about 5% of them, for a profit of about $39 million. As of late February [2006] he had 13.87 million unexercised options left from the October 1999 tranche. His profit on those, if he exercised them today, would be about $717 million more.*
>
> *The 1999 grant was dated the very day UnitedHealth stock hit its low for the year. Grants to Dr. McGuire in 1997 and 2000 were also dated on the day with those years' single lowest closing price. A grant in 2001 came near the bottom of a sharp stock dip.*[1]

As you can imagine, numerous lawsuits were filed alleging wrongdoing by the company and its executives. Dr. McGuire subsequently wrote a letter to shareholders stating, "As soon as we became aware of the criticism, we commenced a thorough review of our historic practices ..." Soon after, they announced nine changes to their current practices including establishment of a set date for the issuance of stock options. The only conclusion that can be drawn from this is that it took the disclosure associated with the article in the *Wall Street Journal* for the executives and board of UnitedHealth Group to recognize that their practice was inappropriate. Might their defense have been, *"Everyone was doing it?"*

STANDARDIZED CHEATING

In their praiseworthy book, *Freakonomics,* Steven D. Levitt and Stephen J. Dubner detail methodologies used to catch teachers who facilitated cheating by students on standardized tests. Clearly, better test scores by their students reflected positively on the teachers in question. In addition, some teachers were actually rewarded monetarily for the recorded improvements in their students' test scores. According to Levitt and Dubner such incentives may be a contributory cause to the apparent rise in such cheating.

The following appeared as the front page headline story in the October 1, 2006, edition of the *Dallas Morning News*. It details the consequences, or lack thereof, for teachers caught cheating in a Dallas area district.

> *On May 12, 2005, Texas education commissioner Shirley Neeley stood in the Wilmer-Hutchins school board chambers and announced the results of her agency's investigation into cheating on the TAKS test.*
>
> *"Twenty-two W-HISD teachers were found guilty of cheating," she said. "The investigation found inexcusable, illegal, unprofessional and unacceptable behavior on the part of these 22 individuals."*
>
> *Shortly after, the Wilmer-Hutchins schools were all shut down. But the careers of the teachers lived on.*
>
> *At least 10 of the 22 Wilmer-Hutchins educators are now working in other North Texas public schools, a Dallas Morning News investigation found. None has faced official sanction, more than 2 ½ years after the cheating took place.*
>
> *Most were able to find new jobs weeks after Dr. Neeley's statements.*
>
> *They were able to do so in part because the body responsible for disciplinary actions against teachers, the State Board for*

> *Educator Certification, has been slow to act on the cases. The agency has a notorious backlog and a reputation for letting cases lie dormant, sometimes for more than two years.*
>
> *In addition, state officials chose not to use their normal method to inform school districts of the findings of their investigation.*
>
> *State officials defend their decisions today. They say that informing schools about the investigation's findings would have likely dissuaded those schools from hiring the implicated teachers. Cheating, they say, is not a serious enough offense to risk that.*
>
> *"Educators have told us that being flagged has a chilling effect on their ability to find employment," said Chris Jones, general counsel for the State Board for Educator Certification. "There needs to be a special justification for us to do that."*[2]

This is another example of people or institutions caught in the cycle of the public's tolerance of unethical behavior. Clearly, our ethical lapses are not isolated to the business sector. The message that is sent to our children is that cheating, if not acceptable, is not reprehensible. Until this message is altered, the behavior we can expect from our children and young professionals may well be disappointing.

STEROIDS

Just as individuals have a responsibility to act with integrity, so do organizations. If organizations turn a blind eye to inappropriate behavior they nurture an environment where "*Everyone is doing it*" becomes an acceptable excuse. Major League Baseball became embroiled in a crisis because league officials and the sports media ignored the mounting evidence that a number of players were using illegal performance enhancing drugs. That lack of oversight resulted in some short term gains, specifically rising fan interest and increased broadcast and endorsement revenues during the chase to break the single season home run record in 1998. However, this apparent "turning a blind eye" led to more widespread use of performance enhancing drugs by some of the game's highest profile players. Major League Baseball now finds suspicion heaped on any player who performs at an extraordinarily high level. The game's most sacred records are being tarnished by the mere question of whether or not the record breaking player cheated. De facto asterisks are found in the minds of many fans, if not in the record books themselves. Players are retroactively judged as they become eligible for Hall of Fame election. Baseball's very integrity has been questioned by those inside and outside the game.

THE SUM OF THE PARTS

If the preceding discussion has not yet convinced you it is in your best interest to behave with integrity, consider the following. During a panel discussion on the topic at one of our firm's meetings, one of my partners said that, "Trust cannot be commoditized." He felt that the long term relationships he built with his clients and the trust that had been built up over the years helped him fend off competitors who claimed to be able to do a better job for less. At the end of the day, clients will choose the professional they feel most confident will perform the task at hand. Over the long haul, most people will not hire consultants they do not trust. Building that trust requires that consultants act with integrity every minute of every day.

THREE

THE LESSONS OF ENRON

The Enron story has been well chronicled. Ultimately it is a story of tragedy and deception. Tragic for not only the innocent victims affected by the collapse, employees, retirees, suppliers of the company, but also for the participants primarily responsible for Enron's downfall. Enron's systemic deception extended to those investors who relied on public representations with respect to the financial soundness of the company.

Enron's collapse is a case study in the human capacity for self-deception. The story is necessarily long and not easily described in a few paragraphs. For those who are interested, I recommend a book entitled, *Conspiracy of Fools*, by Kurt Eichenwald. The author does an excellent job of chronicling the small steps that led participants to commit a spiraling series of acts that were illegal, dishonest and unethical. On page 11 of the prologue to that book, the author summarizes the essence of the story.

> *Ultimately, it was Enron's tragedy to be filled with people smart enough to know how to maneuver around the rules, but not wise enough to understand why the rules had been written in the first place.*[3]

This quote should haunt the leaders of growing, professional services firms, large or small, that are filled with intelligent, highly motivated and ambitious individuals. While it is relatively easy to assure oneself of co-workers' professional capabilities, it is more difficult to know the level of integrity and character that lies beneath the surface. In this day and age, it is possible for a relatively small group of professionals, if not a single professional, to undo all of the good works performed by those before him, with a single dishonest or deceptive act.

This cannot be illustrated better than the sad case of Arthur Andersen. Again, volumes have been written about the downfall of Andersen. After reading much of it, and hearing from some who were directly involved during the downfall, I can only conclude that, at some point they lost their way.

When my wife, Karen, and I graduated from the University of Illinois in 1977, Andersen was the shining light among what were then the "big eight" accounting firms. Based in Chicago, they were known industry-wide for their commitment to quality and professionalism. It is difficult to imagine that in less than 30 years the firm would be reduced to a shell.

RULES OF THE ROAD

In my home city, Dallas, Texas, we have a problem. As I travel around the country, I have come to realize that this is not a problem that is exclusive to Dallas. Rather, it appears to be of epidemic proportions around our nation's metropolitan areas. A few years ago, my daughter, Emily, was studying to receive her driver's permit. One day I picked up her copy of *Rules of the Road*. It said that upon seeing a yellow light, the driver should either stop or proceed with caution. Apparently, due to our need to accomplish more and more in less and less time, some of us are willing to cut corners. More specifically, when we see a light turn yellow, instead of stopping or proceeding with caution, we speed up. The first few times we do this, we make it through the intersection (hopefully) and end up saving a couple of seconds. This emboldens us. We start to try to make it through the yellow light from farther and farther away. Maybe we eventually get a ticket because we didn't quite make it through before the light turned red. Unfortunately, many drivers learn the hard way. They see the light turn yellow and they automatically speed up. Why not, they haven't been caught before? But in the blink of an eye, the car in front of them decides to stop, or the driver in the crossing lane's light turns green and he proceeds into the intersection. The cars crash and sometimes burn. It is not pretty and is often fatal.

I believe that this is exactly what happened to Arthur Andersen. They saw the yellow lights. However, they were seduced by the allure of more and more professional fees. Couldn't this accounting standard be stretched a little? Isn't its meaning subject to interpretation? Maybe we should let the partner in charge of the account decide, instead of the experts back in the main office? When running that first yellow light, fatal accidents are rare. Andersen's missteps, not unlike Enron, were numerous. They ignored a series of yellow lights, until finally, they crashed and burned.

There were professional services firms, other than Andersen, that enabled Enron to perpetuate its fraud upon the public. Many firms have been sued or fined by various oversight agencies. Some have settled. One concept that has emerged from the various court rulings is that, "knowledge and deliberate indifference" is not a valid defense for wrongdoing. This should have a chilling, yet ultimately positive effect on the way professional services firms view the activities and motives of their clients.

I fear, as described in the article from Reuters presented below, that the sum total of our actions over recent years has led the entering generation of business people to believe that "cheating" is an acceptable business practice. Hopefully, they will not have to learn the hard way. Thankfully, the public's expectations of our elected officials and business leaders have been raised.

> *September 20, 2006*
> *BOSTON (Reuters) - Graduate business students in the United States and Canada are more likely to cheat on their work than their counterparts in other academic fields, the author of a research paper said on Wednesday.*
>
> *The study of 5,300 graduate students in the United States and Canada found that 56 percent of graduate business students admitted to cheating in the past year, with many saying they cheated because they believed it was an accepted practice in business.*
>
> *Following business students, 54 percent of graduate engineering students admitted to cheating, as did 50 percent of physical science students, 49 percent of medical and health-care students, 45 percent of law students, 43 percent of liberal arts students and 39 percent of social science and humanities students.*
>
> *"Students have reached the point where they're making their own rules," said lead author Donald McCabe, professor of management and global business at New Jersey's Rutgers University. "They'll challenge rules that professors have made, because they think they're stupid, basically, or inappropriate."*
>
> *McCabe said it's likely that more students cheat than admit to it.*
>
> *The study, published in the September issue of the Academy of Management Learning and Education, defined cheating as including copying the work of other students, plagiarizing and bringing prohibited notes into exams.*
>
> *McCabe said that in their survey comments, business school*

> *students described cheating as a necessary measure and the sort of practice they'd likely need to succeed in the professional world.*
>
> *"The typical comment is that what's important is getting the job done. How you get it done is less important," McCabe said. "You'll have business students saying all I'm doing is emulating the behavior I'll need when I get out in the real world."*[4]

Perhaps, instead, they will take their lead from the individuals described in this article from the September, 2006, edition of *Chief Executive.*

THE REAL THING

> *A Coca-Cola employee and several accomplices managed to pirate a number of confidential documents and a sample of a new product from the company's Atlanta headquarters and tried to sell them to rival PepsiCo for $1.5 million. The scam was dropped in its tracks when the folks at Pepsi told Coke of the attempted heist. Coke called in the FBI, which launched a surveillance and sting operation. An FBI agent posed as a go-between for PepsiCo and nabbed the individuals who attempted to hawk the goods. Coke CEO Neville Isdell even penned a memo to Cokesters praising the erstwhile rival for tipping them off.*
>
> *But there's more to the story than cooperation between competitive adversaries. As industrial espionage goes, the incident hardly rivals Smiley's People, but unreported in the news accounts is the fact that the decision to tell Coke was not an executive one. When I mentioned this incident to PepsiCo CEO Steve Reinemund, he said he was out of the country at the time. When he got the thank you call from Isdell, he wasn't even aware of what happened. PepsiCo's crucial part in the affair was handled by an executive secretary and her opposite number with the company's general counsel. When she received*

the letter offering detailed and confidential information, she understood what was going down and took immediate action. The phone call to Atlanta took place that afternoon. Even other senior executives weren't aware of the incident until later.

When it came to knowing the right thing to do, the folks at PepsiCo needed no instruction, no committee meetings and no executive agonizing. They just did what they knew to be the right thing and told the boss later. It speaks volumes for the Purchase, N.Y., based company and its leadership that a profound ethical sense is so deeply imbued in its culture.

It also suggests how profoundly leadership in business has changed. After enduring headlines accusing CEOs of avarice and self-dealing, it is somewhat affirming to learn that there are leaders who lead by example, and do so in ways that often go unremarked.[5]

Tom Morris was one of the most popular professors at Notre Dame University. His field is philosophy and ethics. If you ever get a chance to hear him speak in person, do not hesitate to do so. You will not regret it. He brings a refreshing view to the issues confronting people today, both inside and outside the business world. The following was extracted from an article Morris wrote:

I think we've forgotten what ethics is really all about. Too many business people these days seem to think that ethics is really just about staying out of trouble. You create lots of rules, and then follow them to the letter, and you encourage others to do so as well, in booklets and memos, all for the sake of staying out of trouble. But ethics has never been mainly about staying out of trouble. The ancients saw it all much more deeply. They believed that ethics is all about creating strength – strong companies, strong relationships,

> *strong people. Ethical behavior creates the foundation for trust, and without trust there can never be effective, efficient partnerships and collaborations of any kind. When people come to think that ethics as just about staying out of trouble, as a functional equivalent – covering their tracks well, maintaining deniability, manipulating accounting rules in complex ways – that leads to disaster.*
>
> *There is also a misconception abroad in the land that, in some relevant sense, business is war, or else is at least a highly competitive mental contact sport, and that anything permissible in war or football is perfectly OK in corporate life as well, aside from, obviously, shooting or physically tackling people. Deception in war, for example, reduces casualties, and in a football game can make all the difference for a first down, or a touchdown. Craftiness has always been seen as a warrior virtue, like courage, persistence, and focus. The quarterback who fakes out the defense can be a hero. But deception in business, rather than reducing harm, can have the absolutely opposite effect, as we've just been seeing. Surprising the competition can be completely acceptable, and even advisable in business, but there are certain sorts of surprises that neither Wall Street nor Main Street likes to see. Many of the warrior virtues, such as courage and persistence, do indeed apply in important ways to business. But others don't. And it's a failure to see the difference that has brought individuals and companies down. Business is a creative, humane endeavor that, for all its competitiveness, requires a level of honesty, public openness, and accountability that should never be compromised for the sake of the game or the win.*[6]

Perhaps our business graduates should be required to sit through one or more classes with the likes of Professor Tom Morris. Learning the minimum legal hurdle may be a prerequisite to graduation from business school. Learning and practicing the "do right" hurdle is a prerequisite to long term success.

FOUR

WHEN THE "DO RIGHT" HURDLE IS UNCLEAR

It is relatively easy to advocate meeting the "do right" hurdle. However, the world is complicated and the right thing to do is not always obvious. In fact, we have seen circumstances when the "do right" hurdle may be contrary to the court's view of the legal standard. The most obvious example of this is a reporter held in contempt of court and sent to jail for failure to reveal his confidential sources.

A couple of real life examples that I know of may be enlightening.

A client bought an undercapitalized health insurance company. The company was losing lots of money because its products were underpriced. One of its policies was issued to 48 policyholders in a particular state. That policy form had lost a substantial amount of money over the prior few years. Upon further review it was found that one of the 48 policyholders had caused the vast majority of the loss. The company had a couple of choices. It could raise the premium each policyholder in the state paid. This would not have fixed the problem as the premiums could not have been raised enough to overcome the continuing losses. They could have decided to cancel all of the policies in that state. This would have eliminated the source of the loss, but would have also left 48 policyholders without coverage. Alternatively, they could have done nothing. The company insured over 40,000 policyholders. If the losses continued, the company risked becoming insolvent, thus risking the coverage of all of its policyholders nationwide.

So, what is the do right hurdle in this case?

Another example. A client engaged us to perform an appraisal of a company he wanted to sell. We performed the appraisal and determined that the value was within a certain range. We sent the appraisal to our client who subsequently sent it out to potential buyers. Later, we found out that, through no fault of our own, one of the underlying assumptions used in our appraisal was false. Changing the underlying assumption would reduce the range of values substantially. We told our client and recommended that we re-issue the report for use by prospective buyers. The client instructed us that we were not engaged to make such a change.

So, what should we do? If we were to re-issue the report and send it to the potential buyers who had received the original report we almost certainly would be sued by our client. In addition, doing so may have been in conflict with professional standards set by the American Academy of Actuaries. At the very least we would lose the client and jeopardize the substantial fee we had earned through the hard work necessary to prepare the reports.

The hard reality is, deciding how to meet the "do right" hurdle is not always clear.

The only helpful advice I can offer you is don't try to solve these dilemmas alone. Discuss them with other professionals whose judgment you trust. In the vast majority of cases, the problems you will face are not conceptually unique. The circumstances may differ, but many of the underlying issues are the same. The old adage that two heads are better than one has never been truer than it is today. Life can be complicated. Seek and accept advice from others you respect when the "do right" hurdle is not clear.

When I give these examples, everyone always wants to know what we decided at the time. In the first example, we were lucky. As so-called "numbers people," we sometimes forget the human element. Upon investigation, we found that the problem causing the losses for the insurance company was acute, not chronic. Thus, the losses were not expected to continue and no further action was necessary by the company.

In the second example, we decided that losing the client was the least of our problems. In fact, based upon the client's response when confronted with the flawed appraisal result, we no longer wished to work for the client after completion of the assignment. We re-issued the report and sent it to the client. We left it up to him to decide whether or not he would forward it to potential buyers. Remember, you are defined by those you associate with, in this case those you choose to work for. As the saying goes, "If you sleep with dogs, you get fleas."

FIVE

WINS AND LOSSES

Even a casual review of the lives of most successful individuals reveals one common denominator. The road to the top is not monatomic. There are many bumps along the way. Setbacks, some severe, must be overcome. Persistence is a common virtue of most successful individuals. The willingness to overcome setbacks is well documented, be it Oprah Winfrey or Abraham Lincoln. It has been well documented that Michael Jordan, perhaps the greatest basketball player in the history of the game, was cut from his high school basketball team. David Halberstam's biography of Jordan, *Playing for Keeps*, documents the day Jordan was cut and his reaction to his coach's decision.

> *But on the day the varsity cuts were announced – it was the big day of the year, for they had all known for weeks when the list would be posted – he and Roy Smith had gone to the Laney gym. Roy Smith's name was on it, Michael's was not.*
>
> *It was the worst day of Jordan's young life. The list was alphabetical, so he focused on where the Js should be, and it wasn't there, and he kept reading and rereading the list, hoping*

> *somehow that he had missed it, or that the alphabetical listing had been done incorrectly. That day he went home by himself and went to his room and cried...*
>
> *Leroy Smith noticed that while Jordan had been wildly competitive before he had been cut, after the cut he seemed even more competitive than ever, as if determined that it would never happen again.*[7]

An individual's character is often most apparent when you see how he responds to adversity.

The silver screen has depicted lesser known sports successes and the travails endured by those participants along the way in such movies as, "*Remember the Titans,*" "*Rudy*" and "*Hoosiers.*"

If you want to succeed, one thing is clear. You must be willing to suffer setbacks and learn from them. Those who choose to stand on the sidelines may never lose, but they will never know the pleasure of winning, either. Perhaps John Wooden, the legendary basketball coach of the UCLA Bruins said it best:

> *Did I win? Did I lose? Those are the wrong questions. Did I make my best effort? That is what matters. The goal in life is the same as in sports: make the effort to do the best you are capable of doing – in marriage, at your job, in the community, for your country. Making the effort is what counts. The effort is what counts in everything. Perfection is what you are striving for, but perfection is an impossibility. Do the best you can under the conditions that exist. That is what counts. You never fail if you know in your heart you did the best of which you are capable. Excellence is the peace of mind that comes from knowing that you did your best to become the best that you are capable of becoming.*[8]

SIX

THE UPS AND DOWNS OF A CAREER

Accepting that you will enjoy wins as well as suffer defeats in your career allows you to keep each of these in the proper long-term perspective. Never getting too high after victories or too low after defeats keeps you focused on the steps necessary to go forward.

I have enjoyed a modicum of success in my career, to date. I have also suffered numerous defeats. The actuarial profession requires that each individual pass a series of examinations in order to attain the designation of Fellowship, the highest level in the profession. These exams are very competitive. Few applicants pass all of them without experiencing failure. I was not one of those few. While it was a wrenching experience at the time, eventually I was able to regain my focus and successfully complete the exam-taking process.

I began my consulting career with Milliman after having been employed as an actuary at a number of life insurance companies following my graduation from college. I opened the Dallas life and health practice for Milliman in the spring of 1986. We had no clients and there were no other employees. The new Dallas practice grew steadily in 1986 and 1987 to the point where there was need for four additional employees by the end of 1987. Even more important, in the summer of 1987 my only child, Emily, was born. Everything was great!

In the spring of 1988 I learned that I had a previously undetected congenital heart defect, something called coarctation of the aorta. Shortly thereafter I underwent open heart surgery. I was seriously ill, my consulting practice was suffering as a consequence and I was responsible for this beautiful newborn baby. Suddenly, things weren't so great.

I worked on Thursday, entered the hospital late that afternoon, had surgery the following morning and was discharged three days later, on Tuesday morning. I couldn't drive for six weeks. However, the Friday morning following my discharge from the hospital, I returned to work. I was determined not to let our practice fail.

Well, thanks to lots of hard work and a little luck, the practice got back up on its feet. Business was flowing in. In the spring of 1989 I was elected a principal of Milliman. Always the loyal fan, I was thrilled that my beloved Fighting Illini had advanced to the college basketball Final Four. Unfortunately, they lost to Michigan, a team they had beaten soundly at the end of the regular season, in the national semifinals. But overall, I had no complaints. Things in my life were going well.

In 1990 I was elected an equity principal (equivalent to full partnership within Milliman's corporate structure). It should have been a time of celebration. Instead, partially due to the Gulf War and ensuing recession but mostly due to a failure to replenish the amortizing asset that was our expertise, business in our practice fell to an all-time low. We buckled down, recovered and eventually expanded. In 1996 I was elected to the board of Milliman and also to the Board of Governors of the Society of Actuaries. As Charles Dickens said in his classic, *A Tale of Two Cities*, "It was the best of times, it was the worst of times." Assuming that there were no transactions pending or assignments due, we typically designate the two weeks surrounding the end-of-year holidays as time-off in the Dallas office.

As I was packing to leave the office for the holidays one of my co-workers came in to tell me two things. First, he and his wife were having marital difficulties. Second, his wife was being investigated by the SEC for stock trades she had made earlier in the year. This piqued my curiosity. As it turned out, my worst nightmare was being realized. Evidently, she, as well as my co-worker's "girlfriend," had purchased stock in a thinly-traded life insurance company for which we were assisting in a possible sale to another publicly traded life insurer. A prerequisite to working in the Mergers & Acquisitions industry is the ability to keep confidential information confidential. If you cannot keep nonpublic information to yourself while assisting with a transaction, you will not work there for long. It is a matter of trust, and it is required by federal statute.

Upon hearing the grim news, the first thing I did was call our CEO to inform him of the situation. We then called the law firm that represents us. The next day they sent an attorney who specializes in securities matters down to our office to determine the facts. I received a phone call from the SEC indicating their desire to ask me a few questions. I said that I had just found out about the situation and asked if we could talk the following Monday morning. They agreed.

That weekend was the longest of my life. I could not sleep. I feared losing the practice that I had worked so hard to develop. After all, who would hire us if we couldn't keep confidential information confidential? Most of all, I feared that Milliman and my friends and colleagues there would be damaged.

Finally, Monday morning arrived and with it the call from the SEC. At least I could set the record straight with them. The call commenced with a reading to me of my constitutional rights. I had not expected this, but in retrospect probably should have. It certainly got my attention. Over two hours of conversation, I explained what had happened. I had told our staff of the potential impending transaction because their assistance was needed by our client, the company that was to be acquired. The individual involved quickly resigned from Milliman and the SEC investigation focused on him. Among other penalties, he lost his professional credentials as an actuary.

I subsequently made telephone calls to more than 15 individuals involved in the transaction. I called CEOs, CFOs, attorneys, investment bankers and other advisors on both sides of the transaction, to inform them of the investigation and to apologize for the actions of the former Milliman employee. These were some of the toughest phone calls I have ever had to make. However, surprisingly, most of the individuals I talked to appreciated the personal update and expressed empathy for what we were going through.

We eventually worked with or for virtually everyone involved in that transaction on subsequent deals. While the entire episode was time consuming and left everyone involved exhausted, we were able to turn what could have been a terrible negative into a positive.

In 2000, I was elected by my peers in the profession as vice president of the Society of Actuaries. At almost the same time I was elected chairman of Milliman. Both are great honors and come with great responsibilities that I take very seriously. These elections represent high points in my career but, as always, challenges were to follow. The post- September 11 period produced a significant drop in business across the consulting industry. Many firms suffered significant lay-offs of professionals. Others ceased to exist or were acquired by their competitors. While we continued to grow as a firm, it was a struggle.

The point of all of this is that over the course of a career you, too, will enjoy many victories and suffer a few defeats, some of which will feel at the time quite debilitating or even fatal. In the words of Winston Churchill, you "never give in, never, never, never, never – in nothing, great or small, large or petty – never give in except to convictions of honor and good sense." Persistence is the single trait that separates those who succeed and those who fail. Celebrate your victories, but never allow yourself to get too high. Learn from your defeats and proceed to the next battle.

SEVEN

THE MOST IMPORTANT DAY OF MY LIFE

On January 8, 1988 Pete Maravich passed away. He was playing basketball with some friends in a church gym when his heart failed. An autopsy revealed a previously undetected congenital heart defect. Maravich was 40 years old. He had been an outstanding college and professional basketball player. His death affected me because, as a child growing up and playing basketball in the 60s and 70s, "Pistol Pete," as he was known to his fans, was one of my idols. Although I was 32 years old at the time, Maravich's sudden passing hit me hard. As it turned out, his death would affect me more than I could know.

I grew up in a small town, northwest of Chicago. I was born with a heart murmur. It was not considered a serious problem and it did not keep me from participating in sports. Also, I had chest pains as a child. At my annual physicals growing up our family doctor minimized these chest pains as "growing pains" and did not consider them serious. In college my blood pressure hovered around 140 over 90, marginally high for someone my age who was not overweight and was generally considered to be in good physical shape. The chest pains continued, but because I experienced such pains continuously throughout my life, my doctors were not especially concerned.

Following Pete Maravich's death, I made an appointment with my general physician who then referred me to a cardiologist. The cardiologist listened to my medical history and took the blood pressure in my arm which was 140 over 90. He then took my blood pressure in my upper leg—90 over 60. Previously I had not had my blood pressure measured in my leg. When I asked whether it was unusual to have two different readings the doctor replied that it was unusual and that I definitely had a problem. The next week, at age 32, I had cardiac catheterization. During a cardiac catheterization a small tube is threaded through a blood vessel into the heart. A liquid dye is then injected into the heart allowing doctors to observe the functioning of the heart muscle. This procedure would confirm the cardiologist's suspicions that I suffered from a congenital heart defect.

It didn't take the doctors long to identify the problem with my heart. It was coarctation of the aorta. In layman's terms, this meant the aorta (the primary artery attached to the heart) was twisted, so that only a portion of the normal blood flow was allowed to pass. This condition is normally identified and corrected early in life. The doctors seemed quite excited to witness the condition in an adult male, as it was quite unusual. I was less enthusiastic.

After the procedure I met with my cardiologist and discussed treatment options. He said that, while not acute—after all I had been living with the condition for over 32 years—he recommended surgery as soon as possible. Absent surgery, he said, surviving to age 50 was unlikely. Given that my only child, Emily, was born the previous summer, there was no question that I would have the surgery.

During the conversation with my cardiologist we talked about Pete Maravich's death. I explained that Maravich had collapsed while playing pick-up basketball and had died soon, if not immediately, thereafter. My doctor asked if I had experienced any symptoms, especially whether I had felt faint during physical activity. I told him I could remember a couple of times when this had occurred. He said that had I fainted I probably would have been dead by the time I hit the floor. I am not sure whether this was true, but I had no intention of finding out. Consequently, on April 8, 1988, I had open-heart surgery to correct a heretofore undetected congenital heart defect. I am now 54 years old. Had Pete Maravich not passed away due to a similar heart defect, I might not be here today.

Given the title of this chapter and the events I have just described, you might assume that the day Pete Maravich died was the most important day in my life. You would be wrong. It certainly was a transformational day in my life, but it was not the most important day.

The day you marry is certainly an important day. For most of us, the choice of a spouse will determine much of our subsequent happiness, or lack thereof. Likewise, the births of your children, particularly your first, are transformational days. However, these experiences are shared by many. We recognize their importance at the time. They are not what I am talking about. Rather I am referring to a singular day, unique to you, that had the greatest impact on your life. You may have experienced it in your childhood. It may have occurred while you were an adult. You may not have recognized its importance at the time.

For me, that day occurred in the winter of 1969, during my freshman year in high school.

Throughout the preceding summer, and the fall of my freshmen year, I practiced basketball daily. My conditioning was excellent, although I was never blessed with outstanding endurance, for reasons that we now know. I excelled during try-outs that year for the freshmen basketball team. When the team members for the "A team" were announced, my name was at the top of the list.

During the first few weeks of practice my relationship with the coach deteriorated. He was a taskmaster and I tried very hard to please him. However, the harder I tried the worse I played. When the day of the first game arrived, while I was in the rotation, my playing time was limited. Consequently, when I entered the game I tried too hard which typically resulted in me making errors. My confidence waned.

The team started the season with five straight wins. I contributed little to them. We lost our sixth game. I didn't play much that game but had played well when I was in. During lunch hour the following day, the coach came up to me in the hall and said that he was not happy with the play of the regulars and expected me to step up and contribute more. I was quite encouraged.

The practice that afternoon was a tough one. The coach was hard on everyone. His approach was to identify one player who was not performing particularly well, single him out, ridicule him, and punish him with added physical exertion. The coach was a bully. We all knew what was coming and didn't want to be the person singled out. It didn't take long for the coach to identify his victim. It was someone who had not played at all during the loss the previous night. The coach's treatment of my teammate was relentless and unfair. Given our talk earlier that afternoon, and my newfound confidence, I raised my hand to ask a question while he was ridiculing the other player, trying to divert attention away from his victim. I was successful in doing so. However, the coach now focused all of his attention on me.

During a three-on-two fast break drill I was on the wing and passed to the man in the middle, who was a step or two behind me. The coach blew his whistle, stopped play, and proceeded to explain to me in very explicit terms that you never throw the ball backwards during a fast break. We repeated the drill. This time, when I looked to pass to the man in the middle he appeared to be a couple of steps behind me so I dribbled in for the layup. The coach found this unsatisfactory and felt I was playing selfishly. We replayed the drill several times; each time with unsatisfactory results as far as the coach was concerned. He was in my face the entire time. Eventually he became so unhappy that we were ordered to line up for dive drills in which two players started at the baseline and, on the whistle, dove for the ball which had been placed on the free throw line. Of course, I was one of the first two participants. Failing to retrieve the ball, I would normally go to the back of the line, waiting to face off with others who had similarly failed. However, the coach made me immediately challenge the next guy in line. And the next guy and the next guy and so on. This drill was quite demanding physically, and doing it over and over made it even more so. I mention this because after the third or fourth attempt the coach really got in my face.

This was the first time I ever remember feeling like I was about to pass out.

The following day I was demoted to the "B team."

It was the most important day in my life.

And, while he probably has no memory of it, it may have been the most important day in the coach's life. What would have happened had I hit the floor dead? At the very least his career as an educator would have been jeopardized, which would have been too bad. He was new to the teaching profession, inexperienced and immature. However, I understand that he eventually became a valuable and contributing member of the school district's administration. His actions as a young teacher could have ruined his career had I died that afternoon.

So why do I believe that the day I was demoted to the "B team" is the most important day of my life?

Ignoring the obvious reason that I literally may not have survived the rest of the season under his tutelage, I changed that day. Whether consciously or subconsciously, I made the decision that I would never again be made to think that I was not good enough. While an honor student before this incident, I became a straight-A student afterward. (This was before grade inflation made such a distinction less meaningful.) I was subsequently driven to succeed in everything that I did. I graduated from the University of Illinois in three and a half years with Highest Distinction. I became a Fellow of the Society of Actuaries at age 25. I became vice president and chief actuary at age 27 at the medium-sized life insurance company where I worked. Three years after joining, I became a principal at the consulting firm where I now work. I was voted to the board of directors at age 41 and named chairman at age 44.

It is important to remember that someone teaching your child may have an effect on him or her that could last a lifetime. At my 10- year high school reunion a number of former basketball players were visiting and catching up with each other. During our conversation, one of the guys asked whether any of us had nightmares from our experiences with the coach of our freshman basketball team. I thought asking that question took a lot of courage for I, too, have had such recurring nightmares. Others mentioned that they had had similar nightmares. Over thirteen years later! My experience has affected how I interact with my daughter's teachers. It has affected how I interact with my daughter and has help make me a better parent. As parents we tend to unconsciously minimize the impact that certain everyday events have on our children's lives. I think often about this particular incident that happened when I was 14 and I remember the profound impact it had on my life.

In many ways, being demoted from the "A team" to the "B team" in my freshmen year shaped my life more than anything else, before or since.

So what was the most important day of your life? Thinking about this one incident may make me guilty of excessive introspection. Being cut from a basketball team at age 14 is certainly not as traumatic as losing a child, spouse or other loved one. Karen, my wife of over 30 years, lost her mother to cancer that same freshman year of high school. If not her most important day, it certainly must rank in the top two or three. I have had friends who lost children at a young age. The effect of that trauma on their lives is unimaginable to me. Fortunately, most of us have not suffered such devastating tragedies.

However, a by-product of such introspection is the realization that I have been truly blessed. Perhaps the process of identifying the most important days in your life will help you to achieve a similar perspective.

EIGHT

LIFE BALANCE

Finding the right balance between your work and your personal endeavors is absolutely necessary if you are to live a fulfilling life. Long-term success on both fronts demands it. Having said that, there are a few things you must understand and accept. First, each person has a unique balance that is right for him or her. Likewise, you may have a different balance at different stages of life. Working 3,000 hours a year for a few years in your early to mid-20s may be acceptable to you, whereas such a workload in your mid-30s may not. You may never want to work that hard, while others may find it fulfilling to do so.

Finding the right balance is your responsibility. It is not the job of your supervisor. It is not your spouse's (although he or she will certainly have some input into the decision). The ultimate responsibility is yours and yours alone. Virtually all firms will allow you to work long hours if you appear willing to do so. You need to communicate to your boss the amount you wish to work. If the firm that employs you doesn't allow you the flexibility to determine your own comfort zone, find one that will. Now, this doesn't mean that you will never have to work when you would rather be doing something else. It doesn't mean that you will never have to alter personal plans at the last minute due to client demands. It **does** mean that over a reasonably extended period you should be able to devote the amount of time to both your professional life and your personal life that makes you happy.

Recognize also, that those who devote more to their professional life will most likely be rewarded financially and proceed up the career ladder more quickly. There are trade-offs associated with the choices you make and the life you wish to live. Find a firm that will accommodate your priorities.

NINE

A CONSULTANT'S MOST IMPORTANT SKILL

Many skills are needed to be a successful consultant. As we have already considered, you must possess expertise that others want to tap. You must be able to effectively communicate your findings through both the written and spoken word. However, I believe the one critical skill that will determine whether an otherwise capable consultant will succeed, is his or her ability to listen. It is also a skill that many consultants have difficulty learning, because everyone thinks he is a good listener.

The genesis of many client/consultant disputes is when the consultant has failed to understand exactly what the client needs from the consultant. What question is he asking the consultant to answer? Clients have little appetite for consultants who try to force a solution down their throats.

Many billing disputes arise, not because the work product is of poor quality, but because the deliverable fails to address the fundamental question the client wants addressed. If you, as a consultant, come into a client meeting with a preconceived notion as to what the client wants and what you will deliver to him, you are at great risk of making this mistake.

Sometimes, it is equally important to distinguish between what the client says and what he really wants. Many times the client knows that he has a problem but isn't sure which questions to ask. Understanding the real issues the client faces is fundamental to adding value to the client.

One of the keys to completing a successful consulting assignment is the ability to identify the ultimate deliverable before beginning the work. I remember one particular client meeting I attended, along with three other consultants from our firm. The sum total of our billing rates approached $1,500 per hour. The meeting lasted approximately four hours. On our way home one of the more junior consultants observed that I had said very little in the meeting, merely posing questions to the client. He questioned whether we should bill the client for the meeting because, in his view, we did not add any value to the client. In fact, the client project proceeded to a successful conclusion, one in which the client was very happy. What the junior consultant was missing was that the initial meeting was critical to defining the issues that the client wanted us to address. Listening enabled us to do so and resulted in us adding substantial value to the client by producing a high quality deliverable.

Recognize that people have different personality traits. Their style may differ from yours. There have been many studies that document this phenomenon and categorize people accordingly. The topic is too complex to address here in detail. However, if you are to be successful, you have to be comfortable dealing with others who have a style other than your own. Part of effective listening and communicating is the recognition that people communicate in varying ways. This is the first step toward effectively communicating with others.

TEN

PERSONAL SKILLS ASSESSMENT

There are four basic job functions that exist within any professional services firm. Possessing the skills necessary to perform any or all of these functions will, to a large degree, determine your level of success. The four job functions are listed as follows:

1. Ability to apply technical skills.
2. Ability to manage those with superior technical skills.
3. Ability to communicate technical results.
4. Ability to generate new business.

The progression from a beginning professional to a partner/principal position within a firm typically requires that you obtain all of the skills needed to perform each of these job functions. Your initial few years will be devoted to honing your technical abilities and obtaining any necessary or appropriate credentials. Some consultants will stop at this point. Others will progress to the point of being able to manage other professionals. If the firm has an "up or out" philosophy those who do not progress to the next level will typically be asked to leave. Generally, such progression is expected to occur within three to five years. The ability to communicate technical results and keep existing clients happy is the next level, and is typically associated with those reaching a "junior" partner status. The ability to develop new business is the final step in the progression and is the primary job function of those who attain full partnership status. You must master the first three skills before you will be effective at generating new business. Clients are quick to identify "empty suits" devoid of any ability to add value to their operations.

The best way to progress up the ladder is to perform the job responsibilities of the higher level position. Once those who make personnel decisions see that you can handle a job with more responsibility, you are more likely to be promoted. Aggressively do more, seek more responsibility, accept additional assignments eagerly. Busy people accomplish more. It is human nature to aspire to the top of the ladder. This is certainly true of the type of goal-oriented individuals who are drawn to consulting. However, it is important to step back and do a self-assessment of not only your innate skills, but also of your desires. Many who aspire to partnership level do not really want to perform the job functions associated with that position. Once elected, they become disenchanted with their new responsibilities. Unfortunately, it is very difficult to climb back down the ladder; the only remaining option may be to leave. As the saying goes, "Be careful of what you want, for you will surely get it."

ELEVEN

MULTITASKING

When it comes to multitasking I have one word of advice for you. Don't. Clients pay for and deserve your undivided attention. Nothing turns them off more than a consultant who appears to have something more important to do or somewhere else he would rather be. Specifically, answering e-mails (a phenomenon of the BlackBerry age) or receiving cell phone calls or text messages during client meetings shows disrespect for your client's time.

Unfortunately, this occurs frequently with less seasoned consultants who are not responsible for business generation and, sometimes, even with longtime consultants who certainly should know better. Always remember how difficult it was to get the client assignment in the first place and communicate your expectations to all consultants assigned to the project. Recognizing the inherent value of a client's time is a great way to avoid sending the wrong message to the client.

It just stands to reason that more careless mistakes occur when you are multitasking. In the litigious age in which we live, such errors can be costly. If you feel the need or desire to multitask, ask yourself one question: would you want a doctor to be multitasking in the middle of your surgery? What about in the middle of a surgical procedure on your child? What about the pilot of the airplane on which you are a passenger?

In his book, *Outliers*, Malcolm Gladwell discusses the genesis of catastrophic mistakes, including airplane crashes:

> *Planes crashes rarely happen in real life the same way they happen in the movies. Some engine part does not explode in a fiery bang. The rudder doesn't suddenly snap under the force of takeoff. The captain doesn't gasp, "Dear God," as he's thrown back against his seat. The typical commercial jetliner – at this point in its stage of development – is about as dependable as a toaster. Plane crashes are much more likely to be the result of an accumulation of minor difficulties and seemingly trivial malfunctions.*
>
> *In a typical crash, for example, the weather is poor – not terrible, necessarily, but bad enough that the pilot feels a little bit more stressed than usual. In an overwhelming number of crashes, the plane is behind schedule, so the pilots are hurrying. In 52 percent of crashes, the pilot at the time of the accident has been awake for twelve hours or more, meaning that he is tired and not thinking sharply. And 44 percent of the time, the two pilots have never flown together before, so they're not comfortable with each other. Then the errors start – and it's not just one error. The typical accident involves seven consecutive human errors. One of the pilots does something wrong that by itself is not a problem. Then one of them makes another error on top of that, which combined with the first error still does not amount to catastrophe. But then they make a third error on top of that, and then another and another and another and*

another, and it is the combination of all those errors that leads to disaster.

These seven errors, furthermore, are rarely problems of knowledge or flying skill. It's not that the pilot has to negotiate some critical technical maneuver and fails. The kinds of errors that cause plane crashes are invariably errors of teamwork and communication. One pilot knows something important and somehow doesn't tell the other pilot. One pilot does something wrong, and the other pilot doesn't catch the error. A tricky situation needs to be resolved through a complex series of steps – and somehow the pilots fail to coordinate and miss one of them.

This is true not just of plane crashes. It's true of virtually all industrial accidents. One of the most famous accidents in history, for example, was the near meltdown at Pennsylvania's Three Mile Island nuclear station in 1979. Three Mile Island so traumatized the American public that it sent the U.S. nuclear power industry into a tailspin from which it has never fully recovered. But what actually happened at that nuclear reactor began as something far from dramatic. As the sociologist Charles Perrow shows in his classic Normal Accidents, *there was a relatively routine blockage in what is called the plant's "polisher" – a kind of giant water filter. The blockage caused moisture to leak into the plant's air system, inadvertently tripping two valves and shutting down the flow of cold water into the plant's steam generator. Like all nuclear reactors, Three Mile Island had a backup cooling system for precisely this situation. But on that particular day, for reasons that no one really understands, the valves for the backup system weren't open. Someone had closed them, and an indicator in the control room showing they were closed was blocked by a repair tag hanging from a switch above it. That left the reactor dependent on another backup system, a special sort of relief valve. But, as luck would*

> *have it, the relief valve wasn't working properly that day either. It stuck open when it was supposed to close, and, to make matters even worse, a gauge in the control room that should have told the operators that the relief valve wasn't working was itself not working. By the time Three Mile Island's engineers realized what was happening, the reactor had come dangerously close to a meltdown.*
>
> *No single big thing went wrong at Three Mile Island. Rather, five completely unrelated events occurred in sequence, each of which, had it happened in isolation, would have cause no more than a hiccup in the plant's ordinary operation.*
>
> *"The whole flight-deck design is intended to be operated by two people, and that operation works best when you have one person checking the other, or both people willing to participate," says Earl Weener, who was for many years chief engineer for safety at Boeing. "Airplanes are very unforgiving if you don't do things right. And for a long time it's been clear that if you have two people operating the airplane cooperatively, you will have a safer operation than if you have a single pilot flying the plane and another person who is simply there to take over if the pilot is incapacitated."*[9]

Lack of focus, fatigue, lack of effective peer review, time pressure, inadequate communication and added stress; at one time or another, each of these has played a role in the missteps for which actuaries and actuarial firms have been held financially responsible.

We hear many athletes talk about being "in the zone" when they are playing particularly well. You don't have to be an athlete to experience being "in the zone." I know other professionals who have experienced a similar feeling during periods of particularly intense focus and productivity. I, myself, have enjoyed such periods. In his article entitled, "Zone Read," Michael Wolf, Ph.D., talks about what it means to be 'in the zone.'

> *The zone is being able to use one's mental capacity to the fullest – fully concentrating, focusing, relaxing and performing without disruption.*
>
> *There have been various traits described to help you know when you are in the zone. The following is a list of some of those characteristics:*
>
> 1. *Your mind is quiet. This means there are no worries being carried over from everyday life. The mind can still focus without effort. Verbal thinking quiets down allowing the brain to perform optimally.*
>
> 2. *You feel unhurried even in the face of pressure.*
>
> 3. *Action and awareness come together. Instead of trying to perform beyond one's capability, there is an integration of an awareness of what one can accomplish and the actions necessary to carry out those commands.*
>
> 4. *There is a feeling of complete control. Essentially, this relates to ironically having control while at the same time giving up control in order to achieve that.*
>
> 5. *Pressure increases focus rather than taking away from it. Your concentration increases in spite of the situation.*
>
> 6. *Self-consciousness decreases while self-awareness increases.*
>
> 7. *There is an absence of fear and anxiety.*

8. *Moving from one thought to the next happens freely and automatically.*

There are also signs to know when you are not in the zone. Essentially these are the opposite of the previously listed traits for knowing when you are in the zone.

1. *You feel rushed and panicked. Time seems to be passing quickly, and you feel helpless to slow it down.*

2. *Sights and sounds around easily distract you. Everything seems to be a distraction and causes you to lose focus.*

3. *You are worried about the outcome.*

4. *A lack of motivation.*

5. *You may try to force yourself to be in the flow.*

6. *Rather than gaining control you try to force yourself to be in control. You may over-think.*

7. *You may be afraid to make mistakes. When this happens, fear sets in, which can be paralyzing.*[10]

Given the potential for distraction and lack of focus, it is difficult to imagine being "in the zone" while multitasking. Incremental errors, wandering focus, an increased potential for client dissatisfaction; what exactly is the upside to multitasking?

TWELVE

COMFORT WTIH AMBIGUITY

Very few of us are comfortable with the ambiguous. It is human nature to want to know all of the rules, up front. To know what the consequences of our actions will be. To know exactly how and when we will be rewarded for our work and good deeds. Laws are enacted by our legislatures to remove ambiguity from our interactions in society. Contracts are formed between individuals and entities, in large part, to remove ambiguity.

Nonetheless, to some degree, ambiguity will always exist. Our ability to not only survive but thrive in ambiguous situations will partially determine how successful we are.

We see people's reactions to ambiguity every day in the way they approach financial instruments. Those seeking a fixed return with a certain maturity date will likely invest in bonds. Those who are uncomfortable with the ambiguity inherent in payments due from less capitalized companies will probably opt to invest in more highly-rated companies. In most investments, reducing the level of ambiguity will also result in a reduced investment return. For example, those who are uncomfortable with the ambiguity associated with investing in highly rated companies may decide to invest in United States treasuries or federally insured certificates of deposit, thereby accepting a commensurate reduction in yield.

Still others, more comfortable with risking when and even if they will be paid, may choose to invest in common stocks with the potential for much greater returns along with the increased possibility of losing one's entire investment.

To some degree, the ambiguity factor plays out in most circumstances of our everyday lives. If you absolutely have to know what your compensation for a particular period will be, you will want to be compensated on a "salary only" basis. However, if you are comfortable foregoing this knowledge and security, you may want to accept a lesser salary with a bonus based upon performance, the sum of which may be greater (or less) than a salary without the prospect of a bonus.

Comfort (or discomfort) with ambiguity extends far beyond what type of investment vehicle you should choose or how you would like to be compensated. Ambiguity reaches everywhere. Actuaries, as a whole, are not comfortable with ambiguity. We develop models to project what is likely to happen under certain circumstances. These models are driven by assumptions which, in turn, are driven by data. Inevitably, the data will be lacking some significant component that would allow us to state an unequivocal conclusion. Unfortunately, our clients typically need the results before the holes in the data have been filled. This creates ambiguity and discomfort. For some, this discomfort can become debilitating.

Acknowledging that ambiguity exists, what can we do to become comfortable with it? First and foremost, accept that it does exist. We cannot eliminate it entirely. However, we can work to minimize it and its effects on us. Every challenge has many moving parts that create uncertainty. Eliminate as many moving parts as possible. Minimize the unknowns. Know the knowable. List the variables. Doing so results in the ambiguity becoming closer to finite and easier to deal with.

Accepting the fact that we are living in an ambiguous world and becoming comfortable (or at least less uncomfortable) with it will differentiate you from the many others who are unable to recognize and accomplish this important task.

THIRTEEN

THE (NOT SO) LITTLE THINGS MATTER

Your actions send signals to others. Specifically, doing what you say you are going to do tells the people you work with that you can be relied upon. Likewise, not doing what you have committed to do sends a very negative message. I am not merely talking about the big things, but rather small commitments as well. Saying I will get back with you tomorrow and failing to do so sends a message that you do not want to send (unless, of course, you no longer want to do business with that person anymore).

PROOFREAD

When you deliver a report with typos, misspellings and poor grammar you are sending a message to your client. Doing so indicates a lack of appreciation for quality. If the deliverable is sloppy, was the work performed in a sloppy manner as well? If typos exist, was the report proofread? Was the work subject to a rigorous peer review process? These are not questions you want your client to ask.

VOICEMAIL

Voicemail is a great tool when used properly. It allows busy people to leave you messages without engaging in an endless round of telephone tag. However, it can be and often is misused by consultants. I know that some time management experts tell you to "turn off the phone and get some work done." Unfortunately, this also sends a message to your clients and prospective clients. Returning calls at your convenience, rather than theirs, indicates that you value your time more than you value theirs. Again, think about how hard you worked to get that call. Do you really want your most valuable client or hottest prospect sent to voicemail? Do you enjoy being connected to a machine when you call for customer service? Having an assistant who answers the phone sends the message that you care about the caller. An assistant will allow you to take the really important calls if you can. An assistant can tell the caller whether you are taking a break down the hall or whether you are out of the country. An assistant can tell the caller when it will be possible for you to return the call. Your assistant will develop a relationship with your clients. Voicemail can do none of these things. Clients like working with successful consultants. Not having an assistant to answer the phone during business hours communicates that you aren't quite there yet. You need to cut corners to save a little expense. That is the wrong message to send.

E-MAIL/TEXT MESSAGING

E-mail and text messaging are also fantastic tools when used properly. They also can be very dangerous when used improperly. Due to their ease of use, you can become very informal in the messages you transmit via e-mail and text. Messages meant for and understood by a specific addressee at a specific time can ultimately be read by others who do not understand the context in which the messages were originally sent. Recognize that these messages are saved and can be read and misinterpreted by others.

It has been my experience that few conflicts are resolved through an e-mail exchange. Unfortunately, the tendency is for participants in such an exchange to have their positions become even more intransigent. Recognize when this is happening and call timeout. Reconvene, either face to face or via telephone to try to understand each other's position and find a compromise everyone can live with.

ACCEPT RESPONSIBILITY

No matter how strict your quality controls and peer review processes, everyone makes mistakes. If you play the game you are eventually going to fumble the ball. Of course, if you fumble it more than you should you won't stay on the first team for long. However, it is what you do *after* you fumble that really counts. Do you try to recover the initiative or do you point a finger and blame someone else? Or, maybe you deny having fumbled in the first place? Oh, what's that you say, "Everyone is fumbling!"

When you make a mistake, accept responsibility, correct it and try to minimize any negative ramifications resulting from your error. Next, do what football coaches do. Review the game film. Ask yourself, "What caused the fumble/mistake? How can I avoid making the same mistake in the future?"

A few years ago an individual sued us claiming that an action we had taken caused him harm. We had, indeed, taken the action that he asserted, but thought that we had received his permission to do so. We had received permission from his employer whom, we presumed, had cleared it with him. In retrospect, we should have actually checked with the individual and received his personal permission to proceed. After more than three years rumbling around the court system, we finally met face-to-face, in an attempt to reach a solution that was satisfactory to everyone. The plaintiffs arrived at the scheduled meeting three hours late. Presumably this was a tactic suggested by the plaintiff's lawyer to make us uneasy. It became clear to me that these "mind games" had been going on between the lawyers on both sides for the three year period since the lawsuit was filed. In my view, this was why we hadn't made any progress whatsoever in settling the claim. It is still not clear to me that his lawyers actually wanted to reach a resolution. Rather, it appeared to me that they were more interested in racking up additional professional fees and had been seduced by the thought of expanding the lawsuit into something much larger than the facts supported.

The meeting finally began with the plaintiff explaining the pain and suffering our actions caused him. During his presentation he began to tear up. While it was difficult for me to imagine, it was clear that his pain was real. We took a break and our group met separately. We decided that I, as chairman of the firm, was going to accept responsibility for our actions, explain that there was no malicious intent on our part, and unequivocally apologize for any pain we had inadvertently caused him. As you can well imagine, this made our lawyers a little nervous.

We reconvened the meeting, and I did just that. During my apology, the plaintiff not only teared up again, he began to sob. His attorney was so shocked at what I was doing, I thought she might faint. A few hours later we agreed to settle the case. All the plaintiff really wanted was an apology. Of course, the attorney also wanted money, which we agreed to pay. It pains me that we had to endure the time, effort, money and management distraction over the prior three years before we settled this case, when all we really had to do was accept responsibility and apologize.

We all make mistakes. When you do, accept responsibility for them. Correct the error. Apologize and move forward.

I DON'T KNOW

The most underutilized phrase in many consultants' vocabularies is, "I don't know." None of us likes to admit that we don't know something. However, clients don't expect you to know everything. Most of the time they expect you to come back to them with an answer after you have had time to think about and perform the research necessary to answer the question. Even if the client does expect an immediate answer, you will only get in more trouble if you try to "fake it." Most people who have reached a level within an organization that has the ability and budget to engage a consultant, also have the ability to detect when someone doesn't know the answer. "I don't know the answer to your question, but I will get back to you shortly," is much more acceptable than the alternative to most clients.

DO YOU THINK? WHAT DO YOU THINK? WHAT DO YOU THINK? WHAT
DO YOU THINK? WHAT DO YOU THINK? WHAT DO YOU THINK? WHAT DO
YOU THINK? WHAT DO YOU THINK? WHAT DO YOU THINK? WHAT DO Y
OU THINK? WHAT DO YOU THINK? WHAT DO YOU THINK? WHAT DO YOU
U THINK? WHAT DO YOU THINK? WHAT DO YOU THINK? WHAT DO YOU T
THINK? WHAT DO YOU THINK? WHAT DO YOU THINK? WHAT DO YOU TH
INK? WHAT DO YOU THINK? WHAT DO YOU THINK? WHAT DO YOU THIN
T DO YOU THINK? WHAT DO YOU THINK? WHAT DO YOU THINK? WHAT D
DO YOU THINK? WHAT DO YOU THINK? WHAT DO YOU THINK? WHAT DO
YOU THINK? WHAT DO YOU THINK? WHAT DO YOU THINK? WHAT DO Y
OU THINK? WHAT DO YOU THINK? WHAT DO YOU THINK? WHAT DO YOU
U THINK? WHAT DO YOU THINK? WHAT DO YOU THINK? WHAT DO YOU T
THINK? WHAT DO YOU THINK? WHAT DO YOU THINK? WHAT DO YOU TH
INK? WHAT DO YOU THINK? WHAT DO YOU THINK? WHAT DO YOU THIN
T DO YOU THINK? WHAT DO YOU THINK? WHAT DO YOU THINK? WHAT D
DO YOU THINK? WHAT DO YOU THINK? WHAT DO YOU THINK? WHAT DO

LEADERSHIP AND MANAGEMENT

THINK? WHAT DO YOU THINK? WHAT DO YOU THINK? WHAT DO YOU TH
INK? WHAT DO YOU THINK? WHAT DO YOU THINK? WHAT DO YOU THIN
T DO YOU THINK? WHAT DO YOU THINK? WHAT DO YOU THINK? WHAT D
DO YOU THINK? WHAT DO YOU THINK? WHAT DO YOU THINK? WHAT DO
YOU THINK? WHAT DO YOU THINK? WHAT DO YOU THINK? WHAT DO Y
OU THINK? WHAT DO YOU THINK? WHAT DO YOU THINK? WHAT DO YOU
U THINK? WHAT DO YOU THINK? WHAT DO YOU THINK? WHAT DO YOU T
THINK? WHAT DO YOU THINK? WHAT DO YOU THINK? WHAT DO YOU TH
INK? WHAT DO YOU THINK? WHAT DO YOU THINK? WHAT DO YOU THIN
T DO YOU THINK? WHAT DO YOU THINK? WHAT DO YOU THINK? WHAT D
DO YOU THINK? WHAT DO YOU THINK? WHAT DO YOU THINK? WHAT DO
YOU THINK? WHAT DO YOU THINK? WHAT DO YOU THINK? WHAT DO Y
OU THINK? WHAT DO YOU THINK? WHAT DO YOU THINK? WHAT DO YOU
U THINK? WHAT DO YOU THINK? WHAT DO YOU THINK? WHAT DO YOU T
THINK? WHAT DO YOU THINK? WHAT DO YOU THINK? WHAT DO YOU TH
INK? WHAT DO YOU THINK? WHAT DO YOU THINK? WHAT DO YOU THIN
T DO YOU THINK? WHAT DO YOU THINK? WHAT DO YOU THINK? WHAT D
DO YOU THINK? WHAT DO YOU THINK? WHAT DO YOU THINK? WHAT DO
YOU THINK? WHAT DO YOU THINK? WHAT DO YOU THINK? WHAT DO Y
OU THINK? WHAT DO YOU THINK? WHAT DO YOU THINK? WHAT DO YOU
U THINK? WHAT DO YOU THINK? WHAT DO YOU THINK? WHAT DO YOU T
THINK? WHAT DO YOU THINK? WHAT DO YOU THINK? WHAT DO YOU TH
INK? WHAT DO YOU THINK? WHAT DO YOU THINK? WHAT DO YOU THIN

FOURTEEN

NORDSTROM OR WAL MART?

Both Nordstrom and Wal Mart are very successful retailers. They understand what their customers want and they deliver it, consistently. While both are retailers, their business models differ substantially.

Notwithstanding the friendly greeting you receive when you enter a Wal Mart, its model is to deliver goods to the consumer as cheaply as possible. They have taken this concept to an extreme in their Sam's Warehouse stores, where their focus is on selling large quantities of merchandise at a low margin.

Nordstrom, on the other hand, is at the opposite end of the spectrum. If either my wife or daughter should enter a Nordstrom store at 8:55 in the evening (5 minutes before their advertised closing time) and want to buy a pair of shoes, Nordstrom will allow them to continue shopping until they have found exactly what they want. Theirs is a high margin, high service, high-value-added business.

Obviously, based upon the success that each of these retailers enjoys, both models can work. The key is understanding which model you have chosen. You can't operate under one model some of the time and under the other model at different times. Few companies succeed with a high margin, low service, low-value-added model, although some have tried.

Consulting typically follows the Nordstrom model. Most successful consultancies attempt to offer high margin, high service, high-value-added. There are implications to this decision. It means that if a client calls your office 15 minutes before closing on Friday afternoon, and wants you to deliver something on Monday morning, you do it if you want to keep that client. You are a high service, high-value-added commercial enterprise. It means that you return phone calls and e-mails from clients and potential clients within 24 hours, even when you are out of the office or on vacation. Basically, it means that you are available to the client when he wants you to be available.

A few years ago, a consultant entered my office close to the time he was supposed to head home. He informed me that he had not yet completed a deliverable for a particular client that the client was expecting early the next day. He went on to make the case, quite convincingly I might add, that the client did not really need the work product that soon and that we could finish it up and get it to him later the next afternoon. Whether due to the lateness in the day or the eloquent case that he had made, I ended up agreeing with the consultant.

I went home later that evening and was bothered by my conclusion. Something wasn't quite right with his argument, but I couldn't put my finger on it. I went to bed exhausted. In the middle of the night I woke up when it hit me. The underlying premise of the consultant's argument was correct. The client didn't need the deliverable first thing in the morning. However, my colleague was concerning himself with the wrong question. Consulting is a high margin, high service, high-value-added business. We cannot and should not address only what the client needs, but also what he wants! Nordstrom does not address whether my wife or daughter need that pair of shoes 5 minutes before they close. An inventory of their closets would certainly call into question their need for another pair of shoes. Nordstrom is only concerned with their desire to have another pair of shoes. Being a high margin, high service, high-value-added commercial enterprise is a 24/7/365 proposition.

Let me be clear on this point. Some may have misinterpreted what I have said. While we are in the business of giving the client what he wants, when he wants it, we are not in the business of necessarily delivering the answer he wants. This is particularly true when the consultant is performing an attest-type function. We are in the business of answering the question that all clients ask, "What do you think?" At the end of the day, they might not like what we think. They may disagree with our conclusions. In such cases, it is important to make sure that we have considered all of the available facts, data and circumstances surrounding our conclusions/recommendations and that we alter them if new information becomes available. However, the client has asked us what we think and we owe him that answer, whether he likes it or not. Some of my best clients have sought advice from others, looking for a particular answer they believed was correct; only to eventually return to seek our advice.

It is also important for us to recognize that despite all of our education, training and experience, we are not always correct. We do the best we can with the information that is available at the time. Business is rarely as precise as we want it to be. Much judgment is involved.

Recognize that people of good will can legitimately disagree on any given issue. It is always a mistake to make such disagreements personal. Almost certainly, such a stance will assure that you never work for that client again.

Another example. A longtime client, well beyond normal retirement age, wanted to find a distressed company that he could purchase, turn around and grow. He had been extremely successful in such endeavors in the past and he wanted the challenge again. He called us and asked for our assistance. Within a short period of time there were a couple of companies for him to consider. Late one Friday afternoon, we met with him and his other advisors to discuss the merits of each possibility. A few of his advisors (also well beyond normal retirement age) questioned the reasoning behind putting capital at risk under these circumstances. After all, a successful turnaround was highly dependent upon the particular skills of my client. Given his age, was it smart to proceed with such a transaction? Why didn't he just relax and enjoy his wealth?

After much discussion, well into the night, we decided to sleep on it and reconvene the following Monday morning. After a long week, I was exhausted and was glad to go home and hit the sack. I fell asleep almost immediately, unencumbered by the issues of the day. At about 3 o'clock on Saturday morning I woke up. No longer exhausted, my mind was racing. Under these circumstances, I can rarely go back to sleep, so I got up, worked out and had some breakfast. At around 5:30 that morning I went to the office. It was the first and only time I had been in the office at 5:30 on a Saturday morning. While I was working through some of the issues that we had discussed with the client the prior night, the telephone rang. I was sure it was my wife, asking what the heck I was doing in the office so early on a Saturday. However, the caller was not my wife. Rather, it was my client. We proceeded to discuss and resolve some of the same issues that we were stuck on the prior night. He eventually bought one of the companies, turned it around successfully, and eventually sold it at a substantial return on his investment. After our conversation that morning, I came to realize that I had crossed an important Rubicon. Not only had I been in the office at 5:30 on a Saturday morning, but a client had called me there fully expecting that I would be there! High margin, high service, high value added.

As hard as it is to develop new business, it always surprises me when consultants voluntarily give up an opportunity to sit in front of a client and demonstrate their capabilities. Specifically, they opt to mail, e-mail or FedEx their work product to the client. A report that is mailed to a client (by whatever means) could end up sitting on the client's desk. He or she may not have the time or energy to sort through it alone. Equally important is that you could jeopardize the collection of the charges incurred in producing the report by sending it.

Why not deliver the report in person? Setting up an appointment to review the results in person is an excellent way to display and practice one's skills and knowledge. Inevitably, questions that need to be answered will arise. Being there as the source to directly address those questions makes for an efficient meeting. Clients will appreciate the time, effort and expertise that was necessary to produce such a report. Presenting the results of an assignment face to face also provides the single, best opportunity to get another assignment. Period.

It is shocking to me how many consultants are consistently late to meetings or cancel previously scheduled meetings at the last minute. Such behavior sends the worst possible message; that you believe your time is more valuable than the client's. On some level, your client already resents the fact that you are being paid a high billable rate. Being late sends exactly the message you do not want to send.

Give clients more than they expect. Again, remembering how hard it is to develop a client relationship, it is always surprising to me when consultants fail to give clients the type of service they did when the business relationship began. I guess this is human nature, but it is dangerous behavior for someone who wants to build a practice that will succeed in the long term. There are times when you will agree to provide your services on a fixed fee basis. This may or may not result in the business being more profitable than on a time-and-expense basis. When time charges exceed the fixed fee because the task proved to be more demanding than when the assignment was initially engaged, you should produce the deliverable with a smile. Act grateful for the business. In such circumstances, you are going to do the work that is necessary. You are not going to let quality suffer even though you will not be paid for every hour that you have worked. It is shortsighted to act resentful. At the very least you should generate positive goodwill with the client. If you act resentful, you will not only perform the work for less than an adequate fee, you risk losing the client rather than creating the goodwill that can and should be generated.

FIFTEEN

GROWTH

Company growth is a topic of much discussion. Some people believe that a company either grows or dies. It is certainly true that many failed companies never managed to grow. However, it is not clear that failure to grow is intrinsically linked to business failure. Certainly, it is difficult to argue against growth as one of many objectives. However, growth as an unconstrained "stand alone" objective is not desirable.

It is important to understand how a professional services firm grows. Basically, there are three ways to grow:

1. Expand the geographic area in which you offer your products and/or services.
2. Take market share from your competitors.
3. Expand the products and/or services you offer.

Typically, a new firm grows quickly through expansion into new geographic areas. Management attempts to replicate current success in one geographic area by expanding into another. In terms of professional services firms, offices/consultants are placed everywhere their services are needed. Because of the newness of the firm, growth in this stage is relatively easy.

Once you have offices everywhere you want them, you may shift focus to taking market share from competitors. This is healthy for the economy and society in general as the cost of providing services to consumers typically declines. The quality of the service improves as professionals realize they can be replaced by their competition. Innovation is often the result, as it produces a competitive advantage that is typically not subject to price cutting.

The third mechanism that can be used to grow is through an expansion of products and/or services. Again, innovation can fuel this growth and lead to competitive advantage. Companies often expand the scope of the products and services they offer through acquisitions. Ideally, these acquisitions create complementary products and services that can be combined with the current portfolio, thus enhancing the value-added of both. One plus one exceeds two. If there are no real synergies in the product/service offerings, and the acquisition is consummated merely for the sake of growth, the tactic typically fails. Professional services firms offering disparate, noncomplementary products and services are difficult to manage and can breed cultural crises.

Finally, all clients are not created equal. Uncontrolled growth can lead a firm to accept clients it would rather not have. A disciplined client selection process is necessary to avoid this pitfall. Growth for growth's sake can be a costly mistake.

SIXTEEN

INDEPENDENT ADVICE AND THE POWER OF DISCLOSURE

Independence is a characteristic claimed by many, if not all, consulting firms. However, independence is a relative state of being.

For instance, can any consulting firm claim to be truly independent when it is being paid by the firm to which it is giving the advice? Will the advice given, in some way, perhaps very subtly, be affected by the very existence of the consulting relationship? Will the advice given be colored by the potential for obtaining subsequent engagements with the client? Is the payment received by the firm contingent in any way on the business outcome resulting, in whole or in part, from the consultant's advice?

Could the ownership structure of the consulting firm affect, or be viewed by others as affecting, the advice given? Certainly, an audit firm would not be engaged to audit one of its own subsidiaries. What if the consulting firm is owned by a parent company that participates in an industry to which the consulting firm provides advice? Can a consulting firm claim independence if one of its professionals sits on its client's board of directors? What if one of its consultants has an ownership interest in a client company or in a company that participates in an industry to which it consults? Can it truly claim independence?

Recall the disastrous miscategorization of subprime mortgages in 2006 to 2008. The independence of the rating agencies responsible for analyzing those mortgage-backed assets was called into question. Did the desire for future business affect their judgment of the risks associated with those instruments? Did the fact that the issuer was paying/retaining the rating agency influence their analysis? That such questions were even asked strongly suggested a flaw in the system that may have contributed to the creation and ultimately the bursting of the "housing bubble" and the emergence of one of the most severe economic recessions in the nation's history.

There are many shades of independence. When a firm claims independence it is important to know exactly what that means in light of current circumstances.

Conflicts of interests, real and perceived, exist in business, in politics and in everyday life. A professional services firm's leaders are responsible for aligning the interests of everyone within the firm to the highest degree possible. Likewise, the interests of the firm and its professionals must be aligned with the interests of its clients. And, all the while, it is important to recognize that perfect alignment of interests is impossible. Consulting firms are commercial enterprises. The clients of consulting firms are usually commercial enterprises or public entities. The desire of a consulting firm to do more and increase its fees creates a natural conflict with its clients, who typically want to receive the best level of service for less. This conflict is inherent in virtually every consulting relationship, and clearly must be managed to the satisfaction of all if the relationship is to continue over an extended period of time.

Other conflicts of interests are more subtle. Consulting firms may concentrate their efforts on serving certain industries. Their clients may, in fact, compete with each other. The skills and insight acquired when working for one client may be used subsequently when working for one of its competitors.

The first step in addressing these potential conflicts of interest is disclosure to the client. Making the client aware of these conflicts ahead of time is essential to avoiding dispute and client dissatisfaction down the road. The client may not like the existence of the conflict and this upfront discussion may be difficult. However, having the same discussion after the client has become aware of the conflict is always more difficult.

Many of the issues in the insurance broker scandal discussed earlier would not have existed had the brokerage firms disclosed to their clients "up front" the methods by which they were to be compensated. The potential for conflict would have been recognized and either (1) accepted by the client or (2) dealt with by adjusting the method of compensation, so that compensation better aligned with the interests of the parties involved. I doubt that the ultimate level of compensation paid for the brokers' services would have changed greatly and no one would have been fined or thrown in jail. Keeping the compensation mechanisms hidden from the clients is what caused the problem.

In this context it may be necessary to define the term "client" very broadly. If the conclusion drawn by any user of the deliverable created by the consultant may be affected by disclosure of any potential conflicts of interest, it is better to disclose the conflicts up front. It is difficult for anyone to accuse you of causing them harm by having a conflict of interest if they were made aware of the conflict and of the actions you were going to take to minimize its potential effects before they engaged you to undertake an assignment or utilized the results of that engagement.

Remember. Disclose. Disclose. Disclose.

SEVENTEEN
MODELS

Actuaries and other professionals rely heavily on the use of models to help analyze and project possible future outcomes. These models are typically very finely calibrated such that they would have replicated historical results. Professionals put so much time and effort into the creation of these models that they sometimes forget they are, in fact, only models, not reality. Models will not necessarily predict the future with the degree of accuracy anticipated by those who create them.

This problem is illustrated very eloquently in the book, *When Genius Failed: The Rise and Fall of Long-Term Capital Management*, by Roger Lowenstein.[11] It details the risks taken by a hedge fund based upon models developed, in part, by Nobel Prize winners. Confidence in the results of the models led the firm to make large financially-leveraged bets. Certain unexpected developments transpired. The outcomes projected by the models were, at best, irrelevant and at worst flat wrong. The book reinforces the importance of recognizing the difference between reality and the modeling of reality.

Risk exists in the "tail" of any probability distribution. Mr. Lowenstein's book should be required reading for any professional involved in the development or use of model output.

Models can be relatively simple. They can also be maddeningly intricate. The more detailed models require substantial input of assumptions as well as formulas. Checking the input can be quite tedious and may not be entirely effective. One method of identifying errors is to break the model's output into understandable pieces. It is easier to have an idea of what the model's output will look like if you break it down into smaller pieces. That way you can more easily identify results that don't make sense and are caused by an error. This sort of "sniff test" of the results can avoid the embarrassment of delivering a flawed product to a client.

Extensive residential mortgage default data has been collected for many decades. The severe level of defaults that resulted from subprime mortgages was not a "tail event" due primarily to a statistical aberration. Rather, the underwriting criteria applied to these historic mortgages were fundamentally different than the criteria that produced the default data in 2006 to 2008. Given the results, it seems clear that this change in underwriting criteria was not adequately reflected in this mortgage rating process.

One explanation that is offered for the increased defaults was the piercing of the so-called housing bubble. Once prices halted their decade-long and seemingly endless climb, home owners were no longer able to refinance their mortgages by accessing the artificially low interest rates that existed during the first few years of their mortgage loans. This illustrates the importance of systematically reviewing the critical assumptions that can drive the results produced by a model. Was it really appropriate to assume that home prices would continue to increase into the foreseeable future? Certainly in retrospect, it was not.

EIGHTEEN

BUSINESS DEVELOPMENT (INCLUDING CENTERS OF INFLUENCE)

Business development, that is the art of securing new clients and more work from existing clients, is a topic that is and has been on the top of every consultant's mind for a long time. Much has been written on the topic. In order to address it in a meaningful way, it is important to step back and ascertain what clients are looking for.

Potential clients are looking for someone who can help them solve their problems. Someone who can give them insight into the issues and challenges that they face. Someone who can produce something for them that they can't produce themselves. Someone they feel comfortable with. Someone they can communicate with freely. Someone they trust.

For the most part, clients are not looking to make another friend. Don't get me wrong; client relationships can evolve into social friendships. However, the client was not initially looking for an additional friend; he was looking for someone who could help him solve his problems.

It is my experience that few relationships based initially upon friendship evolve into client relationships. Rather, it is possible, although not necessary, for client relationships to develop into friendships. It is working long hours together through difficult circumstances that facilitates the development of such friendships, not complimentary tickets to this week's sporting event.

Many professionals new to consulting do not understand this basic tenet. They waste their time focusing on developing the social aspects of a new relationship rather than focusing on the delivery of superior service.

Business development pivots on the possession of expertise that clients need. You must communicate to your potential client base that you possess such expertise. The method by which you do so is largely up to you and depends upon your particular skills and comfort level with certain tactics.

When I started my practice in 1986, I had no clients. While I am very comfortable around people, I was not comfortable making "cold calls." Perhaps I doubted the ultimate efficacy of such a tactic. Perhaps it was because I knew I would not be very good at it. While I recognize that cold-calling works for some, it was not a method that I wished to pursue.

Rather, I decided that I would market my skills on a "wholesale" basis. Specifically, I used the writing of articles and the delivery of speeches as mechanisms to communicate my particular expertise to my target market. If I spoke to 300 people, four of those who had attended might eventually contact me directly to inquire about retaining me for an assignment. These became the people that I would follow up with periodically. The tail of such a presentation may be quite long. While someone might contact me the week after I spoke, someone else might not make contact until five years later. The length of the tail was even more apparent with respect to articles I have written for professional publications. Particularly now in the age of virtually instant communication, the written word lives on for future clients and search engine users. If you pursue the "wholesale marketing" tactic, don't be discouraged if no one calls you soon after you speak or publish. The payback may be deferred.

Successful business development requires delivering when you are given an opportunity. Produce more than expected, and do it with a smile. The endorsement of a satisfied client will do more for your business development efforts than anything else, by a long shot. Word of mouth is very powerful, though it can be a two-edged sword. It can work for you if you deliver superior service, but it can work against you if your work product disappoints.

No matter how much you grow, most of your business will come from existing clients. Given this fact, why would you send a significant deliverable to a client via the mail (be it regular, overnight or e-mail) rather than delivering it in person? I mentioned this earlier, but it's important to remember: The single best time to obtain the next assignment is when you are successfully delivering the results of an existing project face to face. Walking the client through the results helps assure that he or she understands the value that the product represents. This increases the likelihood that you will collect a fee commensurate with your effort and the value your work added to the end product. It also gives you "face time" with the executives who engaged you to help them. Think about how hard you had to work to get in front of those people in the first place. The articles you wrote. The research you labored over. The speeches you delivered. The phone calls you made. Why diminish all that effort by *mailing* the final deliverable? Questions about your report will inevitably arise during or after your presentation. The success of one project can lead to another assignment. No matter how busy you are now, in a few weeks you will wish that you had taken the opportunity to schedule an appointment with your client, discuss the work, answer questions and basically strut your stuff.

There are times when a client assignment does not come directly from the client. Rather, the professionals hired for a particular assignment are chosen, either directly or indirectly, by a third party, someone other than the client. Professionals working for the client, such as attorneys, brokers, commercial bankers, investment bankers, and investment specialists may have the ability to either recommend or directly hire the other professionals that work on a particular assignment. When this happens, they become your target market.

Developing and maintaining a good relationship with these individuals is an important element of business development. Such a relationship is maintained through superior performance once the assignment begins, which reflects well on those who referred the business. Likewise, poor performance has the opposite effect. It is rare that you would get a second chance in those circumstances. Once burned, third party referrers have a long memory.

Likewise, recommending other qualified professionals when you get an opportunity creates enormous goodwill with them. The mistake many beginning professionals make is to focus their efforts on what these centers of influence can do for them. By focusing instead on how you can help others succeed, you make an investment that will likely pay off in the long-term. They will remember your efforts the next time they have a chance to recommend someone.

Ultimately, you must remember that you are dealing with people. If you are difficult to work with, it is unlikely that you will be engaged, no matter how superior your expertise may be. People hire individuals who can do the job – people with whom they enjoy working. High level consulting is a very personal endeavor. If they dread working with you, they are more likely to accept others, with less expertise.

A few general pointers when trying to close the deal:

1. Focus on the client. Do not fixate on the cost associated with the assignment, but rather on the value added by the deliverable.
2. When you have made the sale, stop talking. You have achieved the objective. This is true when you are negotiating virtually anything. Some consultants make the mistake of insisting that the other party follows an identical thought process. Remember: how the parties get there is unimportant. The final agreement is what matters.
3. Sell to people who have the authority to approve or deny a purchase. You are wasting your time if you are focused on individuals who have neither the authority nor the budget to engage you.
4. If you are a young professional, develop relationships with junior executives who have the potential to move up in your client's organization. Chances are they will become decision-makers in the future.
5. Focus on "hitting singles and doubles." You'll eventually hit your share of home runs.

NINETEEN

WHO YOU KNOW

I dislike the phrase, "It is not what you know, but who you know." It is wrong headed in at least two ways. Given our information based society where the answer to almost any fact based question can be answered in seconds over the Internet, knowledge has become commoditized. What you know has become significantly less important than what you can do.

Perhaps a more current version of the old saying would be, "It is not what you can do, but who you know." However, I still do not like it because it is still an excuse for failure.

For those individuals who lack real capability, but have contacts who enable them to "get in the door," it is a temporary justification for not obtaining any marketable knowledge and skills. Such individuals are almost certainly doomed to fail.

For those with marketable skills but lacking the contacts needed to show a client what they can do, it is also an excuse. Earlier, we focused upon developing the skill sets necessary to succeed. This chapter will focus on developing a network of contacts that will give you the ongoing opportunity to show what you can bring to the table.

Getting "in the door" is a critical element of success that is not well-understood by many young professionals. The best proof I can offer of the veracity of this statement is my observations over the years of successful professionals I have had the pleasure to know and work alongside.

These professionals can develop enough opportunities to keep not only themselves but a number of other professionals working on challenging and interesting assignments. The common denominator for these standout individuals is their willingness to nurture others. They go out of their way to help up-and-comers as well as experienced professionals. They treat others with respect and civility. They know that doing so will, over the long run, result in the reciprocal sharing of opportunities. If your recommendation helps another professional get a job or be engaged in an assignment, that person will certainly be grateful and remember you when they have the opportunity to return the favor. However, people also build their network of reliable contacts because they enjoy it!

A lifetime spent helping others results in a large network of allies; people who, years later, can help you get in a particular door. Let me give you a recent example.

A friend of Karen, my wife, mentioned that her son was getting out of the Marine Corps. He joined the Marines after September 11. He became an attorney and worked in the JAG corps. He was quite impressive, but given the economic environment in 2009, he was having a difficult time securing many interviews. Understandably, it is difficult to develop a professional network while serving in Iraq! In my career I have worked with many attorneys and suggested that he send me a copy of his résumé. I received it via e-mail one rainy afternoon while traveling. I spent a couple of hours forwarding it to various attorneys I thought might be interested. Everyone responded, each with varying degrees of interest. One of the attorneys I contacted forwarded the résumé to another lawyer in his firm. That attorney eventually met with the candidate and introduced him to still another attorney who had been a General in the Marine Corps and had left to start his own firm. At the time of this writing they are still discussing the possibility of employment.

This, in and of itself, would make my efforts on that rainy afternoon worthwhile. Assuming the ultimate success of the candidate, of which I am very confident, I will have made a friend of him and of a former General in the United States Marine Corps. One never knows when that will come in handy. However, there is more!

The attorney (I've never met him personally) who made contact with the candidate was playing golf a couple of weeks after indirectly receiving the résumé from me. One of his playing partners mentioned that he needed an actuary and asked if he had any recommendations. He put the two of us in contact, which led to us making a proposal. Our proposal communicated the requisite expertise and we were subsequently retained to do their work.

A true story, illustrative of the power and importance of networking. My generation called it "developing a Rolodex." Today it is called social networking which is facilitated by the constant advances of technology. If you want to be successful, develop, nurture and maintain your contact list.

To answer the original question; in my experience it is **both** who you know and what you can do!

TWENTY

LESSONS LEARNED FROM THE FINANCIAL CRISIS OF 2008

In order to glean meaningful lessons from the devastation wrought on the financial markets and financial institutions in the spring and summer of 2008, a brief history is necessary.

In the early days of the 21st century, the Federal Reserve lowered short term interest rates to stimulate the economy and to counter the harmful impact of the implosion of the "dot com" stock bubble. The low level of interest rates made purchasing a house comparatively inexpensive. Consequently, the demand and price for houses increased. As time passed, these short term interest rates were raised by the Fed. Wall Street and the nation's homebuilders wanted this increased demand for housing to continue. However, rising interest rates made this unlikely. Consequently, Wall Street developed a product known as the "teaser loan." These loans produced monthly payments that were artificially low in the first two or three years, with interest rates and monthly payments increasing substantially thereafter. By keeping the initial interest rate low, the artificially high demand for housing could continue. As long as housing prices continued to rise, the homeowner could refinance the loan before the high rates kicked in a couple of years later. In many cases there was a substantial penalty due if the loans were refinanced, but the penalty itself could be financed if the value of the house had sufficiently increased. This created a steady stream of revenue for the loan originators.

In addition, qualification standards applied to these loans became significantly less stringent. After all, mortgage originators were paid a fee to create new loans. Since these loans would eventually be syndicated into an investment vehicle by Wall Street, the originating company did not have to concern itself with the financial fallout should housing prices stop their precipitous rise or if the buyers were unable to refinance their mortgages once the interest rates were reset. Rating agencies developed models to analyze mortgage-backed assets that consisted of these loans.

The interest rate "resets" in these mortgages typically did not depend on the level of short term interest rates in the marketplace at the time of reset (remember they were set artificially low in the first place to help the buyer qualify for the loan). Instead increases in interest rates of between 500 and 900 basis points were "baked in" to the mortgage loan. Consequently, buyers who purchased a house and paid 3 percent annual interest for the first couple of years were required to pay between 8 and 12 percent after the initial interest rate reset. Alternatively, they could refinance and pay a substantial penalty assuming housing prices continued to rise. Speculators entered the market. Typically, they did not care about the large increase in interest rates scheduled two to three years after purchase since they intended to sell the house for a profit before this increase occurred.

We know now that this contributed to a massive housing bubble that burst in the summer of 2008, causing housing prices to plummet, mortgage defaults to explode, financial institutions to fail, consumer demand to disappear, the availability of credit to evaporate and a recession the depth of which has not been seen for 50 years to emerge.

Of particular interest to many actuaries was the near failure and eventual government takeover of AIG, one of the world's largest insurance companies. The near collapse of AIG was not caused by its insurance operations, but rather by the AIG Financial Products division. This division dealt with many financial instruments including the sale of credit default swaps on residential mortgage backed assets. By selling credit default swaps on assets consisting of residential mortgages the company earned a fee and essentially guaranteed the timely principal and interest payments due on these mortgages. Initially, this business proved quite profitable for AIG. A substantial amount of data existed on defaults on residential mortgages, facilitating the pricing of these products. However, as underwriting standards for mortgages were liberalized, "teaser rate" loans were introduced to the market and housing prices continued to rise, a perfect storm was brewing. Defaults on residential mortgages skyrocketed once the housing bubble burst, resulting in many homeowners being unable to refinance their mortgages and unable to pay the higher interest rates that had come due on their existing loans. This caused massive losses on the credit default swaps sold by AIG's Financial Products division. Collateral for the losses had to be posted. When the company could not meet its growing obligations, the United States government infused capital into the company via the purchase of preferred stock.

So, what lessons can we learn from this unfortunate sequence of events? Many have called for more risk management on the part of large financial institutions. AIG and others have been criticized for making big bets that they could not pay off. It is hard to argue against the need for more risk management. However, it is also worth examining the substantial data that exists with respect to historical residential mortgage defaults. The level of expected losses was well within AIG's ability to pay. Even losses at the extreme edge of the loss probability distribution curve were within their ability to pay.

Life insurance companies typically issue substantially more life coverage each year than the amount of capital they hold. I have been asked many times over my career by non-insurance professionals what would happen to a life insurance company if every one of its insureds were to die? The answer is obvious. The company would fail. However, absent a catastrophe of cataclysmic proportions, that is not likely to happen. Actuaries and life insurers are comfortable making that statement (and remaining in this business) because we have studied historical insured mortality rates.

A few years ago I was in a meeting with a group of underwriters for a mono-line insurance company that had specialized in insuring mortgages. They were considering entering the life insurance field in a similar way. Mono-line insurance companies typically insure against extremely unlikely events. At this meeting, executives from this particular company told me that they were interested only in insuring events that occurred at or beyond the 99th percentile of the probability distribution curve. After my presentation and subsequent Q&A they determined that they knew more about residential mortgage defaults than we knew about mortality.

I have thought a lot about that meeting since the events of 2008. Surely AIG had access to the same data available to the mono-line insurance company. Their mistake in issuing the credit default swaps was not one of recognizing the level of possible loss due to random statistical fluctuation. Rather, it was one of failing to recognize the probable impact of the shift to a new, very liberal underwriting paradigm, along with the issuance of new "teaser rate" mortgage products and their likely effect on default rates. Another variation was the so-called "Ninja Loan," issued to an applicant with no income, no job and no assets. These also became a part of the mortgage lexicon. To draw an analogy, life insurance companies would subject themselves to a similar level of risk if they decided to issue their products only to the least healthy among us.

Along with calls for more risk management, many are recognizing the advantages of increased involvement by actuaries in such efforts. There is no doubt that the discipline and analytical capabilities actuaries possess would improve the risk management process. However, I do not believe that a more extensive involvement by actuaries would have significantly altered the results at AIG in 2008. Again, this financial catastrophe was not due to a statistical fluctuation. Rather it resulted from a radical change in the way mortgages were issued. Perhaps the involvement of an actuary or group of actuaries would have resulted in recognition of this paradigm shift, but perhaps not. Remember, the company had been earning millions of dollars on this line of business. I can tell you from personal experience that it is very difficult to convince an executive of the need to proceed cautiously when he has been making huge amounts historically on a particular line of business. I have been told more than once that I just did not understand, that the rules did not apply to a particular company because they had a "core competency" that others did not have. In fact, the head of the Financial Products unit of AIG made a public statement very similar to this before the catastrophe struck.

Models were discussed earlier in this text. However, it is worth pointing out that one lesson learned from this disaster has to do with models. Models attempt to project results into the future. Consequently, they are dependent upon assumptions pertaining to future events. Given a set of historical data and a perspective as to what may happen in the future, no two actuaries will come up with the same exact set of assumptions. Typically, there is a continuous spectrum of "acceptable" assumptions. One extreme would reflect more conservatism. The other extreme would be more aggressive. All assumptions within this spectrum would be "acceptable." However, it must be recognized that choosing all assumptions at one extreme or the other, although each individually falls in a spectrum of acceptability, will not necessarily produce a model that falls within a continuous spectrum of reasonableness.

An additional lesson to be extracted from this mess is the extreme connectivity one result has to another. This is a worldwide phenomenon. In no particular order, the change in underwriting standards for mortgages and the products offered resulted in an increase in housing prices, which led to a housing bubble which eventually burst, which led to increased residential mortgage defaults, which led to the failure or potential failure of a number of financial institutions, which led to a credit crisis and stock market implosion, which led to a severe recession and increased unemployment in the United States, which led to a world-wide recession, which led to increased credit card defaults, which led to the implementation of tighter credit standards, which led to a decrease in demand for consumer goods and services...

The interconnectivity of the world's economies and the impact this can have on the companies and institutions we serve can no longer be minimized. This leads us to recognize and acknowledge the emerging importance of another risk that has existed, on a substantially lesser scale, for a long time. Specifically, I refer to counter party risk, defined as the risk that the failure of one financial institution will result in non payment of its liabilities and the eventual impairment/failure of other financial institutions. The primary reason for the high level of government intervention in the mortgage crisis was due to counter party risk. Historically, the most significant counter party risk faced by insurance companies was the failure of one of their primary reinsurers. No longer. Financial institutions are tied as much, if not more, on the asset side of the balance sheet today. Increased focus on risk management must include the potential adverse impact posed by counter party risk to an institution or industry.

STARTING YOUR CAREER THE RIGHT WAY

T DO YOU THINK? WHAT DO YOU THINK? WHAT DO YOU THINK? WHAT D
DO YOU THINK? WHAT DO YOU THINK? WHAT DO YOU THINK? WHAT DO
O YOU THINK? WHAT DO YOU THINK? WHAT DO YOU THINK? WHAT DO Y
YOU THINK? WHAT DO YOU THINK? WHAT DO YOU THINK? WHAT DO YOU
U THINK? WHAT DO YOU THINK? WHAT DO YOU THINK? WHAT DO YOU T
THINK? WHAT DO YOU THINK? WHAT DO YOU THINK? WHAT DO YOU TH
HINK? WHAT DO YOU THINK? WHAT DO YOU THINK? WHAT DO YOU THIN
T DO YOU THINK? WHAT DO YOU THINK? WHAT DO YOU THINK? WHAT D
DO YOU THINK? WHAT DO YOU THINK? WHAT DO YOU THINK? WHAT DO
O YOU THINK? WHAT DO YOU THINK? WHAT DO YOU THINK? WHAT DO Y
YOU THINK? WHAT DO YOU THINK? WHAT DO YOU THINK? WHAT DO YOU
U THINK? WHAT DO YOU THINK? WHAT DO YOU THINK? WHAT DO YOU T
THINK? WHAT DO YOU THINK? WHAT DO YOU THINK? WHAT DO YOU TH
HINK? WHAT DO YOU THINK? WHAT DO YOU THINK? WHAT DO YOU THIN
T DO YOU THINK? WHAT DO YOU THINK? WHAT DO YOU THINK? WHAT D
DO YOU THINK? WHAT DO YOU THINK? WHAT DO YOU THINK? WHAT DO
O YOU THINK? WHAT DO YOU THINK? WHAT DO YOU THINK? WHAT DO Y
YOU THINK? WHAT DO YOU THINK? WHAT DO YOU THINK? WHAT DO YOU
U THINK? WHAT DO YOU THINK? WHAT DO YOU THINK? WHAT DO YOU T
THINK? WHAT DO YOU THINK? WHAT DO YOU THINK? WHAT DO YOU TH
HINK? WHAT DO YOU THINK? WHAT DO YOU THINK? WHAT DO YOU THIN
T DO YOU THINK? WHAT DO YOU THINK? WHAT DO YOU THINK? WHAT D
DO YOU THINK? WHAT DO YOU THINK? WHAT DO YOU THINK? WHAT DO
O YOU THINK? WHAT DO YOU THINK? WHAT DO YOU THINK? WHAT DO Y
YOU THINK? WHAT DO YOU THINK? WHAT DO YOU THINK? WHAT DO YOU
U THINK? WHAT DO YOU THINK? WHAT DO YOU THINK? WHAT DO YOU T
THINK? WHAT DO YOU THINK? WHAT DO YOU THINK? WHAT DO YOU TH
HINK? WHAT DO YOU THINK? WHAT DO YOU THINK? WHAT DO YOU THIN
T DO YOU THINK? WHAT DO YOU THINK? WHAT DO YOU THINK? WHAT D
DO YOU THINK? WHAT DO YOU THINK? WHAT DO YOU THINK? WHAT DO
O YOU THINK? WHAT DO YOU THINK? WHAT DO YOU THINK? WHAT DO Y
YOU THINK? WHAT DO YOU THINK? WHAT DO YOU THINK? WHAT DO YOU
U THINK? WHAT DO YOU THINK? WHAT DO YOU THINK? WHAT DO YOU T
THINK? WHAT DO YOU THINK? WHAT DO YOU THINK? WHAT DO YOU TH
HINK? WHAT DO YOU THINK? WHAT DO YOU THINK? WHAT DO YOU THIN
T DO YOU THINK? WHAT DO YOU THINK? WHAT DO YOU THINK? WHAT D
DO YOU THINK? WHAT DO YOU THINK? WHAT DO YOU THINK? WHAT DO
O YOU THINK? WHAT DO YOU THINK? WHAT DO YOU THINK? WHAT DO Y
YOU THINK? WHAT DO YOU THINK? WHAT DO YOU THINK? WHAT DO YOU
U THINK? WHAT DO YOU THINK? WHAT DO YOU THINK? WHAT DO YOU T
THINK? WHAT DO YOU THINK? WHAT DO YOU THINK? WHAT DO YOU TH
HINK? WHAT DO YOU THINK? WHAT DO YOU THINK? WHAT DO YOU THIN

TWENTY ONE

THE THREE THINGS INTERVIEWERS WANT TO KNOW

When you interview for a job, be it right out of school, later in life or when you are trying to get an initial engagement from a new potential client, there are three things that people want to know about you. These are also the three things that you should want to know about them.

CAPABILITY

The first category of questions that all interviewers want answered is, are you capable? Are you intelligent? Can you learn new things? The reality is, school teaches skills that allow you to learn what you need to know to do the job. Do you have the skills, knowledge and expertise necessary to perform the job? For instance, no matter how motivated you are and how much integrity you have, being an attorney (or doctor, accountant, teacher, actuary) requires a certain level of grey matter. Likewise, being a basketball player in the NBA requires a certain level of natural athletic ability. These natural abilities certainly do not guarantee success. However, an absence of the basic abilities needed to perform a certain job function, be it dunking a basketball or articulating an argument, casts severe doubt upon the prospects for future success. Again, the basics are necessary but basics alone are not sufficient to guarantee success.

Likewise, capability is one of the questions that you should be asking of your future employers. Are they capable? Will they be around for a long time or will they go out of business leaving you high and dry? Is the company's management capable? Times and circumstances change. Have they demonstrated an ability to adapt to changes?

TRUST

The second category of questions that all interviewers will ask concerns your character. Can you be trusted? Do you have integrity? Will you do the right thing, even when no one is looking? The actions of a company's employees are a direct reflection of the company. Are you someone a company would be proud to have as an employee?

Again, these are also questions you should be asking of the company. There are two ways company management can fail. They can be incompetent or they can be dishonest. Either way, the company's chances of succeeding are severely diminished.

COMMITMENT

The third area of questions that all interviewers ask concerns your level of commitment. Are you passionate about succeeding in your chosen endeavor? The world is very competitive. Are you willing to pay the price to excel? We have all heard stories of the type of commitment it takes for top athletes to succeed. Basketball legends Michael Jordan and Scottie Pippen worked out each day before breakfast at Jordan's house. This was *before* the regular team practice.

Two of the 50 greatest players in NBA history, who won six NBA championships together, practicing twice as hard as anyone else.

For many years, Karen and I have regularly attended the US Open Tennis tournament. One day it was quite rainy. We went out to the stadium hoping that the rain would eventually subside. It didn't. But what we witnessed that day left a lasting impression upon us. There, in the pouring rain, on the outer courts, were some of the top tennis players in the world, hitting with their coaches. Practicing. Getting better at their craft. Do you have that kind of commitment to your profession? That is what an interviewer is trying to find out.

That level of dedication, it is exactly what you want to know of a prospective employer or client. Will they pay the price to succeed, or are they merely a temporary player?

TWENTY TWO
WHY GRADES MATTER

I am often asked if grades received in school matter. By now you should know that my definitive answer is "yes." Why do grades matter? I believe there is a direct correlation with two of the three questions that all interviewers ask. Specifically, grades help to answer the first question, (Are you intelligent?) and the third question, (Are you passionate about your chosen field of endeavor?) If you received poor grades you may be intelligent and passionate, but when given the chance to prove it, you didn't. Absent some other compelling attribute, you become a high-risk bet. Since the interviewer's success or failure will ultimately be tied to yours, the chance that you will be hired diminishes. If you did poorly in school, the question you will have to address in your interview becomes:

Are you average, or did you underperform?

Unfortunately, there is no good answer to this question. However, let me be clear. We are not talking about the one semester aberration in which you did poorly because you had a case of mononucleosis. We are talking about a discernible, consistent level of underperformance. Successful people tend to succeed (to the degree capable) in everything they do. Teachers generally don't give C's and D's to those who made a legitimate effort, even if you are not particularly skilled in a certain area. Making C's and D's in your area of concentration indicates either a lack of underlying talent or lack of passion for the subject matter that is necessary for long term success.

Bottom-line: Grades matter. However, does this mean that your life is over if you underperformed in school? Of course not. It does mean that you will probably work a little harder in your initial job search. It does mean that it is time to rev up the engines and focus on the task at hand. Likewise, the fact that you received good grades in school means only that you will be afforded more initial opportunities. You will still be required to perform once you get an opportunity. Your success or failure in life will be a reflection of what you did after you finished your formal education.

TWENTY THREE

THE IMPORTANCE OF READING

Earlier, I commented on the importance of being able to effectively communicate the results of your engagement. Whether writing or speaking, the ability to communicate is a core requirement of all successful consultants, and regular reading will improve communications skills. I am not talking about reading a "how to" book on written or verbal communication. Rather, I am suggesting that merely experiencing how others communicate through the written word will improve your ability to do so. It has been my experience that those who read voraciously with comprehension, can also write. They know how it is done. Their vocabulary expands. They become more articulate. They are not intimidated at the prospect of reading a voluminous report, a necessary evil of consulting.

Please understand, I am not talking about merely reading technical pieces in your chosen field of expertise. Rather, I am talking about reading from a broad array of sources: literature, the classics, fiction, nonfiction, biographies, magazines, newspapers, trade journals. Clients want their consultants to be on top of developments within the industry to which they consult. Nothing turns off a client more than an uninformed, out of touch consultant.

Peggy Noonan, former speech writer for Presidents Reagan and Bush and most recently a columnist for the *Wall Street Journal* once wrote, "One of the greatest professional gifts of my life was a bit of offhand advice given me about 20 years ago by a writer who said, 'Never feel guilty about reading, it's what you do to do your job.' If he hadn't said it, I don't know if I'd read less or read guiltily, but I'm grateful I haven't felt I had to do either."[12]

Read, as much as you can, as often as you can.

TWENTY FOUR

TRAVEL INTERNATIONALLY

The United States has been the growth engine of the world's economy during my working lifetime. However, this is changing. Eventually, given their booming population growth, India and China will join the United States in driving the world's economy. If you are a young professional, this means that you will, at a minimum, have to become comfortable with traveling and doing business outside of the United States. Accept these opportunities eagerly. You should seriously consider any opportunity you have, particularly early in your career, to spend a year or two working overseas. Doing so can only open more doors for you in the future.

TWENTY FIVE

THE VALUE OF THE INTERDISCIPLINARY APPROACH

I have found that some of the most successful consultants are those who possess a basic working knowledge of other professions. For instance, actuaries who have a basic knowledge and understanding of accounting can help their clients bridge the gap between two areas that can cause confusion. Similarly, a basic understanding of our legal system makes a nonlegal professional all the more valuable to his clients. A working knowledge of the use of technology has become a must for all professionals and can help differentiate you from the rest of those in your profession. The advancements in medicine, with their consequent improvements in longevity, have the potential to change society in a very substantial way; these changes will soon touch the work of many professionals.

Additionally, the most successful consultants have a basic understanding of all aspects of the businesses they serve. Specifically, they grasp not only the technical aspects of the pricing of products, but the competitive constraints surrounding the establishment of a price for a product. They understand the sales process. They have insight into how their efforts fit in with the overall strategy of their client.

Does this mean that you have to be an expert in each of these outside areas in order to succeed in your chosen profession? Of course not. However, taking a couple of courses in these or other disciplines at the undergraduate level can only help you achieve a broader understanding of the context in which you will practice your profession. For those consultants currently in practice, it means that time spent learning new things can only help you serve your clients. It also keeps you open to new ideas and allows you to extrapolate challenges and advances in other professions to your chosen profession.

It is a fact of the consulting life; those who acquire a basic understanding of the concepts underlying the work of other professions typically acquire a better understanding and appreciation of how much they do *not* know. That can help you steer clear of trouble.

Conclusion

Individuals drawn to the consulting profession are typically highly motivated, goal-oriented people who are driven to succeed. The commitment required is substantial, but the rewards are great. One final word of caution. Do not allow success in your professional life to become an excuse for deficiencies in other areas of your life. Commit to excellence in all areas of life; as a parent, a spouse, a friend, a partner, a son or daughter, as a citizen. Maintaining a balance will not only help you in these areas, but will contribute to your long-term success as a professional.

END NOTES

1. Forelle, Charles, and James Bandler. The Perfect Payday; Some CEOs Reap Millions by Landing Stock Options When They Are Most Valuable; Luck—or Something Else? *Wall Street Journal, Eastern Edition,* March 18, 2006. Copyright 2006 by Dow Jones & Company, Inc. Reproduced with permission of Dow Jones & Company, Inc.

2. *Dallas Morning News.* 2006. Cheating Hasn't Hurt Teachers: Accused W-HISD Educators Hired in Other Schools. October 1. Reprinted with permission of the Dallas Morning News.

3. Eichenwald, Kurt. 2005. *Conspiracy of Fools: A True Story.* New York: Random House, Inc.

4. Business Grad Students Most Likely to Cheat: Study. *Reuters.com,* September 20, 2006. All rights reserved. Republication or redistribution of Thomson Reuters content, including by framing or similar means, is expressly prohibited without the prior written consent of Thomson Reuters. Thomson Reuters and its logo are registered trademarks or trademarks of the Thomson Reuters group of companies around the world. © Thomson Reuters 2009. Thomson Reuters journalists are subject to an Editorial Handbook which requires fair presentation and disclosure of relevant interests.

5. Donlon, J.P. 2006. Editor's Note: The Real Thing. *Chief Executive,* July/August. Used with permission of Chief Executive © 2009. All rights reserved.

6. Morris, Tom. The Ethics Scandals of Our Day. *Morrisinstitute.com.* Reprinted by permission Tom Morris, philosopher, chairman of the Morris Institute for Human Values and author of such books as *If Aristotle Ran General Motors* and *If Harry Potter Ran General Electric.*

7. Halberstam, David. 1999. *Playing for Keeps: Michael Jordan and the World He Made.* New York: Random House, Inc.

8. Venuto, Tom. A Commitment to Excellence. *IronMagazine.com.*

9. Gladwell, Malcolm. 2008. *Outliers: The Story of Success.* New York: Little, Brown, and Company. Reprinted by permission.

10. Wolf, Michael. 2009. Zone Read. *Avid Golfer,* January.

11. Lowenstein, Roger. *When Genius Failed: The Rise and Fall of Long-Term Capital Management.* New York: Random House, Inc., 2000.

12. Noonan, Peggy. A Year for the Books: Mother Teresa's Secret, and Other Revelations from 2008. *Wall Street Journal*, December 26, 2008.

INDEX

A

B

C

D

S

T

V

W

Z